G. F. (George Forrest) Browne

The Conversion of the Heptarchy

Seven Lectures

G. F. (George Forrest) Browne

The Conversion of the Heptarchy
Seven Lectures

ISBN/EAN: 9783744661041

Printed in Europe, USA, Canada, Australia, Japan

Cover: Foto ©ninafisch / pixelio.de

More available books at **www.hansebooks.com**

THE CONVERSION OF THE HEPTARCHY.

SEVEN LECTURES

GIVEN AT St. PAUL'S

BY THE

RIGHT REV. G. F. BROWNE, B.D.,

BISHOP OF STEPNEY, CANON OF ST. PAUL'S.

PUBLISHED UNDER THE DIRECTION OF THE TRACT COMMITTEE

LONDON:
SOCIETY FOR PROMOTING CHRISTIAN KNOWLEDGE,
NORTHUMBERLAND AVENUE, W.C.; 43, QUEEN VICTORIA STREET, E.C.
BRIGHTON: 129, NORTH STREET.
NEW YORK: E. & J. B. YOUNG & CO.
1896.

PREFACE.

THE story of the conversion of the several kingdoms of the Heptarchy has naturally some points common to the history of two or more of the kingdoms. This has made it impossible to avoid repetition in some cases.

In one respect the subject has been more pleasant than that of last year's lectures (*Augustine and his Companions*). There was scarcely any intervention of Rome in the period dealt with this winter, and it has thus not been generally necessary to enter upon controversial matters. One of the "church" newspapers, in the course of an appreciative review of last year's little volume, made a severe remark on the unnecessary raising of controversial points. But, with one exception, the controversial remarks had a fair connection with the subject; and, without any exception, they had reference to objections and difficulties of modern times, about which, and the need of meeting them, I probably know as much as my kindly critic.

There is another side to the question, and, possibly, to the meaning of my critic. The Roman aggression, which began on the death of Cardinal Manning, is in full play; more full and systematic than persons ordinarily informed know. I am clear that the duty of members of the Church of England, who have the opportunity, is to point out quite frankly the relative weakness of the Roman position, and the relative strength of ours, on the main subjects of the Roman attack upon us. There is a suicidal policy in vogue in some quarters, and perhaps my critic is one of its victims, which is guided by the mistaken idea that if we hold our peace on these points, "re-union" is more likely to come. "Re-union" on any terms which we can accept and which are not fatal to the structure of the Roman claims never can come. The only hope for any sort of "re-union" is that we should frankly and firmly expose the hollowness of the Roman claims.

CONTENTS

	Page
I. NORTHUMBRIA	9
II. WESSEX	40
III. EAST ANGLIA	68
IV. MERCIA	97
V. THE EAST SAXONS	132
VI. SUSSEX, AND CONCLUDING REMARKS .	159
VII. THE BEWCASTLE CROSS, AND OTHER MONUMENTS	188

LIST OF ILLUSTRATIONS

		Page
1. CROSS-SLAB OF OIDILWALD	. . .	151
2. TOMBSTONE (? OF CEDD)	. . . .	152
3. BEWCASTLE CROSS, SOUTH SIDE	. .	191
4. BEWCASTLE CROSS, WEST SIDE	*Frontispiece.*	
5. SUNDIAL AT KIRKDALE	. . .	195
6. RUNIC GRAVESTONE AT THORNHILL	.	205
7. RUNIC GRAVESTONE IN WIRRAL	. .	206
8. CROSS-SLAB AT JARROW	. . . .	207
9. DEDICATION-STONE, JARROW	. . .	209
10. THE CROSS OF THE HOLY JAMES	. .	216

LECTURE I.

NORTHUMBRIA

Subjects of previous courses.—Death of Edwin.—Reign of Oswald.—The Scotic Church.—Aidan.—Death of Oswald and accession of Oswy.—Death of Aidan.—Conference at Whitby.—Withdrawal of the Scotic Church, and estimate of its work.—Development of bishoprics in Northumbria.

Two years ago we dealt with the history and condition of Christianity in these islands before the coming of Augustine[1]. We saw that two hundred years at least before Augustine came in 596, Christianity had, roughly speaking, spread over the whole of the territories which we now call England and Wales, and the south of Scotland; that before his time, Christianity had spread over large parts of the island which we call Ireland; and that, at one time and another, still before the arrival of the Italian missionaries in Kent, Christian missionaries, British and Celtic, had made their mark in large districts of the territory which we call Scot-

---

[1] *The Church in these Islands before Augustine*, S.P.C.K.

land north of the Forth. We saw that in the years between 400 and 596, while there had been progress in many of the parts of these islands, there had been, so far as we can judge, a complete disappearance of Christianity from all parts of the country we call England, excepting the south-west and the north-west; that is, from all parts in which the English invaders of the lands of the Britons had established themselves, whether Angles, or Saxons, or Jutes. But I am myself more and more inclined to think that the Britons were not so nearly extirpated in the English parts as we suppose, and that among the remnants of the enslaved Britons there were remnants of the Christian faith.

Last winter we dealt with the restoration of Christianity in one of the seven kingdoms which the English had set up, the kingdom of the Jutes in Kent[1]. We saw the little kingdom of Kent pass through the relapse into or towards paganism, which marks the story in so many of the English kingdoms; and we considered its final establishment in the faith. With the conversion of the kingdom of Kent we have nothing more to do.

[1] *Augustine and his Companions*, S.P.C.K. Lectures II, III.

Augustine and his companions made sure work there.

We dealt, also, with the introduction of Christianity among the East Saxons, our Essex and Middlesex[1], with their capital—so far as they had one—in ruined London[2]; and we saw it expelled by the sturdy pagans our predecessors[3]. We shall not see its restoration till forty years of darkness have passed; and even then we shall see yet another relapse into inveterate paganism.

We had to glance incidentally at the early existence of Christianity among the East Angles, our Norfolk and Suffolk and parts of Cambridgeshire, and we shall take up the story in that kingdom.

In the great midland kingdom of the Mercians and Middle Angles, in the slowly increasing kingdom of the West Saxons, i.e. all westward from the border of Sussex, and in the isolated kingdom of the South Saxons, our Sussex, we had seen no signs of any renewal of Christianity, since the expulsion of the Christian Britons, or of their Christianity, by the pagan English.

---

[1] So far as I know, we have very little information about the Middle Saxons.   [2] See pp. 147, 155.
[3] *Augustine and his Companions*, S.P.C.K.   Lecture IV.

In the great kingdom of Northumbria, our Yorkshire, Durham, Northumberland, and Scotland up to the Forth, with a generally vague western boundary and great masses of Britons on the other side of the boundary, we saw the planting of Christianity from Canterbury by Paulinus, and his very rapid success. And we saw the whole swept clean away by a combination of pagan Middle Angles and Christian Britons; agreement in political hatred uniting, not for the first or the last time, those who in religion were at complete variance [1]. At that point we broke off.

I propose to begin this winter where last winter we left off, taking up first the history of Northumbria at the death of its first Christian king, Edwin. He was killed in battle at Heathfield, probably near Doncaster, on the twelfth of October in the year 633, fighting against an army of invaders of his kingdom, pagan English and Christian Britons.

The period which these lectures are meant to cover, so far as it can be covered in the time, is, roughly speaking, from 633 to 668. It is hoped that next year the period 668 to 710 may be dealt with; and then those who

---

[1] *Augustine and his Companions*, S.P.C.K. Lecture IV.

live to 1897 will be ready to keep, with appreciation and knowledge, the thirteen-hundredth anniversary of the foundation of the English Church. To keep that deeply interesting anniversary with due discrimination, it will be necessary to be quite clear as to what of our earliest Christian history flowed directly from the work of Augustine and his companions, and what did not. We shall see, as the story unfolds itself in one kingdom after another, and reveals the blended sources of our conversion to the faith, that it would be easy to assign to Augustine too high a place in the full planting of the English Church. And on the other hand, it is most unfair to attempt to dethrone him from the place that rightly is his. Sent by Gregory, he was the first man to convert an English kingdom; and thus Gregory and Augustine founded the Church of the English.

Edwin of Northumbria, as we saw last year, was a very powerful king, ruling over both parts of the great kingdom of Northumbria, the southern Deira and the northern Bernicia. He had been an exile in youth; had recovered his father's kingdom of Deira; had driven out of Bernicia his brother-in-law's family, and reigned there in their stead. When he was killed in 633, his own cousin

Osric succeeded of right to Deira, while Eanfrid, the oldest son of the dispossessed king of Bernicia, succeeded of right to that kingdom. Osric had been converted by Paulinus. The exiled Eanfrid and his brothers had found shelter among the Picts, and there had been converted to Christianity and baptized by the monks of Iona. Thus the Christian Edwin was succeeded on each of his thrones by a Christian, the one looking to Augustine's school of Christianity, the other to the Scotic school. By "Scotic" I mean of Irish origin, whether found in Ireland, in Scotland, or at Iona [1].

But the overthrow of Christianity, and the triumph of paganism, had been for the time so complete, that the two young kings almost immediately apostatised, and returned to paganism. This did not long preserve them in their kingdoms, for Cadwalla, king of the Christian Britons, pursuing his great victory over the English of the north, slew them both within the year. As Bede tells us, the

---

[1] It is scarcely necessary in these days to say that the Irish were the people meant by the word "Scots" in the times of which we are speaking, and that the modern geographical use of the word "Scotland" only dates from the 11th century.

apostasy of Osric and Eanfrid was so much resented by the Northumbrians of his time—he lived from half a century to a century after the event—that they did not count them kings, but reckoned the year as part of their successor Oswald's reign. To Oswald, pagan, exile, Christian, king, martyr, saint, we must now come.

We shall have on other occasions to mention the relapse of kingdoms and kings into paganism, as we have already more than once had to do. But I am not sure that English people realise the fact that for parts of the years 633, 634, and 635, two hundred years after the first coming of the English as conquerors, and many years after the complete establishment of all the seven kingdoms of the English, the Britons reconquered the largest kingdom of all, Northumbria; and that kingdom was actually ruled over by a Christian British king, representing the Christianity of the British Church. The ancient race and Church, which the pagan English had hemmed in among the mountain fastnesses of Wales and Cumbria, had now broken its bonds. Its warriors covered once more the plains of Yorkshire, and the hill country of Durham and Northumberland, and the fertile country of the Lothians, where for so long the Britons had flourished before the Angles came and carved out the kingdoms of Bernicia and Deira. A British Christian king was once more seated in the great natural fortresses of Dunedin and Dungueirn, Edinburgh and Bamborough. But he was there as a Briton, rather than as a Christian. He had no idea of the conversion of the enemies of his race. His aim went no futher than their slaughter.

It did not last long. Eanfrid's brother Oswald succeeded to his rights as King of Bernicia, and he determined to enforce them. In all probability his Pictish relatives supplied him with troops, for, as I have elsewhere pointed out[1], Eanfrid when in exile had married a Pictish princess; their son Talorcan, Talore mac Ainfrit in the Irish annals, was King of the Picts north of the Forth and Tay. With his army, described by Bede as small, but strengthened with the faith of Christ, as Bede says, apparently forgetful of the fact that the British foe were hereditarily Christians—Oswald advanced upon the forces of Cadwalla and completely overthrew them, at a place called in the English tongue of that

---

[1] *Lessons of Early English Church History*, p. 80. S.P.C.K.

time Denises-burna, Denis burn. The name was still in use after 1200. It is probably Dilston near Hexham. This was in 635.

Oswald, we are told, on the night before the battle, had a hole dug in the ground, in which his soldiers fixed a large wooden cross, Oswald himself supporting it while they filled in the earth. Round this they knelt, and prayed for deliverance from the proud and ferocious Briton. Bede does not make any reference to Constantine's vision of the Cross in the heavens, with the legend *in hoc signo vinces*, "in this sign thou shalt conquer," although it would have been quite in his method to do so, if Oswald had had any such meaning. I cannot but think, nevertheless, that Oswald had this meaning, and that the fact was well known. Thirty-five years after this, a very noble cross of stone, originally about seventeen feet high, was set up in Northumbria[1] in memory of a nephew of Oswald, to which I shall have to make further reference later on. The inscriptions on this cross are the earliest examples we have left of the English language. The prin-

[1] At Bewcastle. See my *Lessons of Early English Church History*, p. 99, S.P.C.K., and Lecture VII. in the present volume.

B

cipal inscription begins with the words *this sigbecn thun,* "this slender sign or token of victory," with direct reference, I cannot doubt, to Oswald's triumph, and, I should suppose, some reference indirectly to Constantine's victory. A vision, by the way, Oswald had, according to Adamnan. The blessed Columba himself appeared to him, and promised him the victory.

Oswald found no ecclesiastical organisation. Paulinus had fled, with Edwin's widow and children; and at Rochester he remained, wearing in a manner most irregular, according to the false ideas of later times, the belated pall, which reached him after his flight. The idea of two palls in use, one at Canterbury by an archbishop, and one at Rochester by a suffragan of Canterbury, is enough to confound all the Roman theories of the importance and meaning of the pall, developed since Gregory's time. To Paulinus Oswald did not apply for help. Political and ecclesiastical reasons made that impossible. Paulinus represented the interests of the children of Edwin, on whose kingdoms Oswald had now entered; and Oswald's training was entirely Scotic. Besides, Paulinus had left the bad example of founding nothing solid. He could preach, convert, baptize ; he could not found. There was neither church, nor altar, nor cross, in all Bernicia, set up by him : that is Bede's statement. James, the deacon of Paulinus, stayed steadily at his post, called from him Akeburgh[1], near Catterick. He was the only sign left that Bernicia had been a Christian land in Anglian times ; and even he was in Deira.

To the Scotic Church, then, his nursing mother in the faith, Oswald applied. They sent to him one of their bishops. He, like all the bishops of the Scotic Church other than those in Ireland, was subject to the Abbat of Iona, on the ground that Columba, the founder and ruler of their ecclesiastical province, was a priest, not a bishop. This bishop soon returned from Northumbria, and reported that he could make nothing of the English ; they were intractable, hard, barbarous : just what the runaway Italians had said of Kent. A council was held at Iona, to consider what the next step should be. A member of the council, Aidan, observed that the bishop appeared to have expected too much at first, to have expected to make them suddenly perfect Christians. It would have

[1] See Lecture VII. in this volume.
[2] Called Corman by Hector Boethius.

been better to obey the apostolic precept, "treat them as infants in the faith, feed them with the milk of easier doctrine." We might imagine that the 1260 years from 635 to 1895 were blotted out, and Aidan was telling us how to deal, and how not to deal, with the people in some parts of the east end of London. The council saw that this was a man of discretion, and a man who had formed a plan. They had him consecrated, and sent him to Oswald. Whether because the king and the bishop wished to keep clear of the arrangements made by Edwin and Paulinus; or because Oswald's hereditary connection was with Bernicia, not with Deira, with Northumberland, not with Yorkshire; or because Aidan, like so many of the Scotic missionaries, had a preference for an island; the bishop's seat was set on the island called by the British Medcaut or Medgoed, and by the Angles Lindisfarne. It lies on the coast of Northumbria, in full view of the royal Bamborough; an island at high tide, but at low water separated from the mainland only by sand and a small and shallow stream. The reasons suggested above for the choice of Lindisfarne as the bishop's seat have been given by one writer and another, and are in themselves natural and obvious. The real reason for the arrangement made by Edwin and Paulinus, as it seems to me, was that Edwin's principal residence was near York; that York was the most famous place in the North of England, from a secular point of view, had been the ecclesiastical centre of Christian organization till times then comparatively recent, and was protected by great Roman walls; and that Edwin placed his bishop as near his own chief residence as he could. Oswald, on the other hand, made his principal residence at Bamborough, and he too placed his bishop as near him as he could, in a natural fortress, with the sea and the shifting sand for walls.

However this may have been, the succession of bishops of York was broken off short with Paulinus, and was not resumed till thirty years had passed away. The succession of bishops of Lindisfarne now began. It has not been broken since, except by geographical changes. From Aidan there followed fifteen bishops of Lindisfarne; then seven bishops of Chester-le-Street; then bishops of Durham, sixty to our own Canon Lightfoot, and sixty-one to his friend and successor Dr. Westcott, now the eighty-third from Aidan.

Under Aidan's teaching, Oswald and his kingdom prospered greatly. The king extended his dominion over all the three peoples whom his borders touched, the Britons, the Scots—that is, the Irish settled in the west of North Britain—and the Picts. He won Lindsey back from Mercia. More important still, he was politic enough to weld together the people of Deira and the people of Bernicia, so that in his time there was a cessation of the old jealousies, which broke out again, however, in the next reign. Bede points out that he was happily circumstanced for effecting this useful change, being the son of the former king of Bernicia, Ethelfrith, and the nephew of the former king of Deira, Edwin. But inasmuch as there had been deadly hostility between the cousin-lines of Edwin and of Ethelfrith, and the Anglo-Saxons of those times generally shewed a complete disregard of the ties of consanguinity when dynastic considerations pointed to such disregard, it may be that Bede assigns too much importance to this double descent. Certainly in the previous reigns the relationship had meant bloodthirsty feud.

It is very tempting to enlarge upon the noble character of Oswald, and to tell some of the many pleasant stories about him. But it must suffice to say that his piety made an impression on the popular mind which never died out. Aidan found him a fellow-worker of great value, for he knew the Irish language well; and when Aidan, who knew but little English, preached to the military leaders and attendants of the king, Oswald interpreted to them the heavenly word[1]. How important a part he played in the conversion of Wessex, we shall see when we come to deal with that kingdom.

The news of the progress of the Gospel in Northumbria soon reached the Scotic Church. With that missionary spirit for which they were remarkable, priests and monks of the Scotic Church came in large numbers to Northumbria, and covered the land with Christian teaching. Those of the Scotic missionaries who were priests, Bede specially tells us, administered the sacrament of Bap-

[1] It is only among the courtiers that we hear of this interpreting. There is a good deal to be said in favour of a wider knowledge of Gaelic among the common people in Northumbria than is quite consistent with the supposed obliteration of the Britons. In those early times, the Irish Gaelic and the British Gaelic had not fallen so far apart as not to be easily intelligible, each in the other's land. The next page or two mention facts which are not easy to explain on any other supposition.

tism. Churches were built at the various centres of teaching. The people joyfully flocked to hear the word of God. By the king's good offices property and lands were given for the establishment of monasteries. The English, young and old, were trained in the principles and practice of the regular discipline, for it was especially the monks that came over as missionaries. It is worth while to notice, in view of some modern arguments with regard to church property, and the relations between churches and monasteries in the earliest times, and the origin of parish churches[1], that Bede in this passage clearly makes the building of churches quite a separate thing from the establishment of monasteries, and mentions it as a primary matter of obligation. Also, from another point of view, it is well to notice that if we press Bede's words literally, some at least of the Scotic missionaries were not monks; that is, there were, at that time, seculars connected with the Scotic Church[2].

[1] See the argument in Lord Selborne's *Ancient Facts and Fictions concerning Churches and Tithes*, which tends to shew, incorrectly, as I think, that the monastery church was the normal origin of the parish church. See also p. 35.

[2] Nam monachi erant maxime qui ad praedicandum venerant. Monachus ipse episcopus Aidanus. *H.E.* iii. 3.

CONVERSION OF NORTHUMBRIA. 25

Bede describes for us the manner of life of Aidan. He lived as he taught others to live. He neither sought nor loved this world's goods, but delighted in giving to the poor whom he met whatever the king and the great men gave to him. He moved about the country, in populous and sparsely peopled parts alike, on foot, not on horseback unless some real necessity compelled him. Whenever he saw wayfarers approaching, whether rich or poor, he went up to them at once; if they were unbelievers, he begged them to receive the faith; if they were believers, he strengthened them in the faith, and urged them by word and deed to alms and good works.

So unlike the laziness of Bede's time, a hundred years later, as Bede tells us, was the course of Aidan's life, that he and his companions, whether tonsured or lay, were bound to read the Scriptures regularly and learn the psalms. This was the daily duty of all of them, wheresoever they might be. On the rare occasions when Aidan was invited to a banquet by the king, he took with him one cleric, or two, and after a slight meal made haste to leave, that he and they might occupy themselves in reading and prayer. By his example, religious men and women were brought to fast till three in the afternoon on Wednesdays and Fridays, except during the Easter remission. When rich men did wrong, he never abstained from rebuking them on any ground of respect for their position or fear for himself. He never made presents to great men; only gave them food if they were his guests. Any money he got from rich people, he gave as has been said to the poor, or employed in redeeming such as had been unjustly sold as slaves. Many of those whom he thus redeemed he took afterwards as his scholars, instructing and strengthening them till he brought them up to the priesthood. The instruction of youth was an important part of his work. Indeed it would seem to have been part of his original plan; for we read that when first he was made bishop he had twelve English boys put under his charge, to be instructed in Christ. One of these, Eata, became Abbat of Melrose, and trained Cuthbert. Chad also was one of Aidan's scholars; but whether one of these twelve is not sure.

Oswald reigned only eight years, technically nine, if we reckon to him the year of the apostasy; eight years full of busy Christian work, including the completion of the stone church of St. Peter at York, which Edwin had left breast-high. You can lay your hand to-day on the Anglian wall, if you know where to go in the crypt of York Minster. He was killed in 642, by the same pagan Penda of Mercia who had killed Edwin nine years before. His brother Oswy succeeded, and appointed as the ruler of Deira one of Edwin's relatives, Oswin, son of Osric the apostate; thus, as it would seem, opening the way for a renewal of dissensions between the two parts of the kingdom. Deira prospered greatly under Oswin, and he was greatly beloved. But jealousy between king and sub-king broke out after seven years into open war, and Oswy treacherously put his sub-king to death. Oswin was one of Aidan's greatest favourites, and is very highly praised by Bede for his piety and devotion. The concluding paragraph of Bede's panegyric is worth giving in full. "The King Oswin, moreover, was comely and tall; pleasant of speech, and courteous in manner; open of hand to all, whether noble or not noble. Thus it came about that all men loved him for his royal dignity of mind and look and character, and men, even the most noble, flocked to his service from other provinces. Among his great qualities of valour, and moderation, and peculiar sweetness, greatest of all was his humility." Bede's narrative shews, indirectly but clearly, that though Aidan's seat was at Lindisfarne, and he worked principally in the kingdom of Bernicia, he did in fact cover the whole of the Northumbrian ground; working with the sub-king in Yorkshire as well as with the chief king further north.

When the time came for Aidan to die, in 651, only twelve days after Oswin, he was at his own church at Bamborough. It is still called St. Aidan's Church. This, with some bits of land adjoining, was the only property belonging to him personally, and he seems to have had no residence on the spot. As his illness developed, and it became clear that he could not be moved to his cell at Lindisfarne, they made for him a lean-to against the west wall of the church, which in that neighbourhood is the sheltered side. Supporting himself on a beam placed as a buttress for the church, in this rude episcopal palace, the prototype of Auckland Castle, he died. The beam, it is needless to say, wrought miracles, and resisted the violence of fire.

Aidan had built churches in many places, but not, it would appear, at Lindisfarne. His successor Finan built a church there, of dimensions suitable for the episcopal see; and after the Scotic manner he built it not of stone but of oak, and thatched it with reed. The dedication Bede does not tell us: there is a complete absence of knowledge as to the Scotic dedications in Northumbria. When the other school of thought prevailed, the dedication was changed, if indeed it had any special dedication, or any name other than Finan's church, or the church of the holy Finan, or the house of God. Theodore of Canterbury, when he came north, dedicated it to St. Peter. In another respect it underwent change. Eadbert, seventh bishop of Lindisfarne, took off the reed thatch, and completely covered both roof and sides with plates of lead.

In Aidan's time it was a well-known fact that he observed the Scotic rule for calculating Easter, not the rule which had become nearly universal. But the respect felt for him was so great, that no one cared to stir the question; especially as King Oswy was devoted to the Scotic usages, and his son Alchfrith, who ruled in Deira, was in his youth a favourer of the same side. And when Aidan died, and Finan succeeded, and held the bishopric of Lindisfarne for ten years, political affairs of the highest importance, to which we must refer when we deal with the kingdom of Mercia, absorbed the attention of Oswy and of Alchfrith. When Colman succeeded in 661, the question came to the front. A Scot, converted to the catholic method of calculating the incidence of the Easter festival, Ronan by name, a name which appears both in hagiology and in modern fiction, argued with Colman and his people, and converted many to the true method. Oswy's Queen Eanfleda, Edwin's daughter, had naturally been always on that side. Alchfrith the sub-king, influenced by Wilfrith, had now come over so completely that he had turned out from Ripon the Scotic monks to whom he had given an estate there, Eata the abbat, Cuthbert the hospitaller, and the rest; and had put Wilfrith and his monks in their place. Bishop Agilbert, who had left Wessex because the king there had subdivided his bishopric[1], was living in Northumbria; and he, though he had studied long in Ireland, was a Frenchman, with French consecration, and kept the truer Easter. Romanus, Eanfleda's Kentish chaplain, of course was on the same side. James the deacon, a companion of Paulinus, the only

[1] See Lecture II.

one of his party so far as we know who did not run away when Edwin was killed thirty years before, he had always continued to observe the truer Easter. Agilbert's priest Agatho was another notable person on that side. On the other side was the chief king Oswy, who thought nothing could be better than the Scotic usages of his youth; Colman of Lindisfarne; Hilda of Whitby; and Cedd, our East Saxon bishop, who was paying one of his visits to the north when the matter came to a head.

The question was fought out in free discussion at the famous synod or conference of Whitby in 664, Cedd acting as interpreter between the Scotic and the Anglian sides, and Wilfrith being the principal orator. The result was that Oswy decided against his own personal views. The effects were very far-reaching. It was the turning point in the early ecclesiastical history, not of Northumbria only, but of by far the greatest part of the land of the English. The parts of England which had been converted by the Scotic Church ceased to hold the position of insular isolation given to them by Celtic teachers, and England was no longer divided against itself on points of usage. Our own

East Saxon Bishop Cedd, who receives high praise from Bede for his skill and care as interpreter between Scot and Anglian, between insulator and catholic, loyally conformed to the catholic use. Colman would not change his views or his practice. He and the whole of his Scotic monks left Lindisfarne, taking with them some thirty English monks besides. The English settled at Mayo in Ireland, the Irish at Inisbofin. They had found it impossible to live together in Ireland: for the Irish monks, now they were at home again, wandered about in the summer time while the English gathered the harvest; and then returned for the winter to live on what the English had collected. When Bede wrote, about three-quarters of a century later, Mayo was still an Abbey of English monks, who lived by the labour of their own hands, in much continence and singleness of life.

Though the Scotic Church was thus dispossessed of its hold on Northumbria, the land received yet another Scotic bishop. It is here that Bede mentions the interesting fact, that the south of Ireland was catholic in practice, unlike the north. The south was in direct communication with Gaul, as we know from other sources, and to this we may with much probability attribute the less isolated ways of that part of the island. However that may be, the south of Ireland adopted the catholic reckoning of Easter thirty years before the events of which we have been speaking, in 633. A bishop had come over to Northumbria from the southern province of Ireland, Tuda by name, during Colman's tenure of the bishopric; and had taught diligently both by precept and by example. He was presumably Anglian by birth, his name seems to indicate that; he had been taught and consecrated bishop in south Ireland [1]; he had the coronal tonsure, according to the custom of that province, and held the catholic use of Easter. He succeeded Colman as Bishop of Lindisfarne. The abbacy of Lindisfarne was given by Colman's request to Eata, as being one of Aidan's own pupils. Eata had been turned out of Ripon by Alchfrith some time before, for refusing to conform to the catholic use, but he had now, it would seem, conformed. He ruled the remnant of the Anglian brotherhood of Lindisfarne, now that all the Scots were gone and thirty of the English brethren. There was

[1] See Lecture II.

thus a continuity in the monastic life, though there was a complete and final break in the Scotic succession of monks. This is a point of much importance, when we have to consider the deeply interesting question of the school of art of Lindisfarne.

Thus ended the episode which Bede describes as the thirty years' episcopacy of the Scots—that is, the Irish—in England. He concludes his account by a highly appreciative description of their life and work, of great value as coming from one who was in the most determined manner opposed to their usages. When they left Lindisfarne, he tells us, it was found that they had been exceedingly frugal in their life. There were only just dwellings enough for their own actual needs. They had no property but cattle. They had no preparation for receiving important people; for such came only to pray and hear the word of God. The king himself was wont to come with only five or six attendants, and to leave when his devotions were ended. If by chance he needed food, he was content with the daily fare of the brethren; and their whole care was for the heart, not for the stomach. Thus it was that the religious habit was held in great veneration in those times. Whenever a cleric or a monk appeared, he was received with joy by everyone, as being the servant of God. If they met him on the way, they ran to him, bent the neck, and joyfully were signed by his hand or blessed by his voice. Careful attention was given to the exhortations of the clergy. On Sundays people flocked eagerly to the church, or to monasteries, to hear the word of God. I would again call attention to the clear line drawn between the church, as the first place, and monasteries as the second[1]. If a priest came to a village, the villagers quickly came together to seek of him the word of life. For the clergy had no other purpose in visiting the villages, than to preach, baptize, visit the sick,—in brief, care for souls. They were so free from the vice of avarice, that they refused to receive lands and property for establishing monasteries, unless some great layman forced them to do so; and that practice prevailed in the churches of Northumbria for some time after their departure.

We know from other writings of Bede. especially his letter to Archbishop Ecgbert,

---

[1] See p. 24.

that throughout this description he is drawing a contrast most unfavourable in each respect to the practices of his own times, in which he found and lamented great degeneracy. Verily the epitaph of the Scotic Church in Northumbria, drawn by a hand devoted to the Roman usages, is a testimony to virtues so valuable, that one is almost inclined to minimise the enormity of keeping Easter once in a long series of years while others were keeping Palm Sunday,—if that had been all. Our own rule for Easter is so far from ideally correct, that the late Professor Adams, who took a great interest in the question, used to tell me that he could name a fixed day in April which in the long run would give a much higher average of accuracy, in relation to the Paschal Moon, than our present variable Easter gives, with all its many inconveniences.

We can now leave Northumbria, established in the Christian faith. I hope in a later lecture to say something of material remains, still existing, of the time of which we have been speaking[1]. It must suffice now to add that immediately after the Synod of Whitby

[1] See Lecture VII.

the bishopric of York was re-established, as the bishopric of Deira, Lindisfarne continuing to be the bishopric of Bernicia. Fourteen years later, in 678, Hexham was made an additional bishopric in Bernicia, and Ripon (for one turn) in Deira [1]; and three years later, in 681, Whithorn in Galloway was made a bishopric for the extreme north-west of the expanded Bernicia. Finally, the successes of Ecgfrith, Oswy's son, among the Picts of the East, in Fife, East Perthshire, and Forfarshire, were so considerable, that an Anglian bishopric was established for the Picts, with its seat on the safe side of the Forth, at Abercorn. The slaughter of Ecgfrith in Perthshire or Forfarshire in 684 put an end to the Anglian sway over the Picts, and Trumwine withdrew from Abercorn, the first and the last Anglo-Pictish bishop. In our own time, the sees of the Province of York are as follows:— York and Durham, the origin of which we have sketched; Carlisle, added in 1133, originally a British territory the ecclesiastical government of which was given to St. Cuthbert by king Ecgfrith; Chester, also a British territory, reckoned as belonging to Mercia

---

[1] Bede iii. 28.

and in early times even giving its name to the Mercian see[1], made a bishopric in 1541; and Ripon (1836), Manchester (1848), Liverpool (1880), Newcastle (1882), and Wakefield (1888). Nottinghamshire, till lately part of the northern province, is now embodied in the new see of Southwell (1884), and is reckoned in Canterbury. Sodor and Man had nothing to do with Northumbria.

Not even the misconceptions of a controversial spirit can really question the fact that the Christian Church in Northumbria was built up by the steady painstaking work of the Scotic Church. James, the deacon of Paulinus, had quietly stuck to his work near Catterick, at Akeburgh[2]; but he was one man. The feet of them that published the Gospel of Peace at large were Scotic feet. And, as we shall see in other lectures, the great political position of Oswald and Oswy enabled them to introduce Christianity from Northumbria into other kingdoms of England. In this way, and to this extent, the great bulk of England was brought to the Christian faith mainly through the influence of those who had learned all they knew from the

---

[1] See Lecture IV, p. 126
[2] See Lecture VII.

Scotic Church. To Aidan also we must attribute the introduction of the ministry of women into the Northumbrian Church. He consecrated Heiu, the first nun, the foundress of Hartlepool.

The figures of Oswald and Aidan and Ceadda (Chad) will sparkle in the great windows of our transepts at St. Paul's; the one in the window of the twelve primary Christian kings of English kingdoms, the other in the window of the twelve converting bishops. Edwin and Paulinus will be their companions.

LECTURE II.

WESSEX

Wessex became the supreme kingdom.—Early Wessex.—Birinus.—Cynegils.—Oswald.—Coinwalch, relapse.—Agilbert.—Wini.—Eleutherius.—Isle of Wight.—Subdivisions of the Wessex dioceses.

THE kingdom of the West Saxons, Wessex, was founded by Cerdic about the year 519. It became eventually the most important of all the kingdoms, for it gradually drew to itself all the others, and its kings became kings of England. Every step of Queen Victoria's descent from Cerdic is as well known as her descent from George III; and as the descent of Cerdic from the real personage Woden was carefully preserved, the Queen's descent from Woden is completely known. The same is true of many thousands of the men and women of to-day. The marriages of royal princesses with great nobles, in the middle ages, in England and more especially in Scotland, has given royal descent to a very large number of families, and with royal descent a share in the records of the successions from Cerdic and from Woden.

In the time of which we are to speak, Wessex had not attained to the geographical dimensions which it had when it became supreme. Its southern boundary was the sea, and was therefore unchangeable, except so far as the Isle of Wight was concerned. A vast forest, which hedged in the South Saxons, was a barrier to progress eastward as far north as the latitude of Winchester, though at times the King of Wessex obtained lordship over the South Saxon kingdom. After the battle of Wimbledon, which added Surrey to Wessex, the kingdom of Kent completed the eastern boundary. To the west, the Britons still held their own and barred further progress; so that in the time of King Cynegils, in whose time the knowledge of Christ came, the West Saxons had probably not passed the eastern borders of Wilts and Dorset. To the north, they had possession of Oxfordshire and parts of Buckinghamshire, with, it is said, even parts of Bedfordshire; along their northern border they came in contact with the great central kingdom of Mercia. It is evident that a kingdom thus situated must be exposed to fluctuations of boundary. They had as militant neighbours all the races then in England, Britons, Saxons, Jutes, and

Angles; and any political ferment among any of these told promptly upon Wessex. Some of the West Saxon kings had been most vigorous fighters, and had not confined themselves to the races named. Under the year 597 the Anglo-Saxon Chronicle tells that in that year "Ceolwulf began to reign among the West Saxons. And he fought continually, either with Angle-kin, or with Welsh, or with Picts, or with Scots."

Somewhere about the year 633, when Honorius of the Italian mission was Archbishop of Canterbury, and Rochester, left without a bishop for six years, had just received the fugitive Paulinus as bishop, and there was no other bishop of the Italian mission in all England besides, only the Burgundian prelate Felix at Dunwich, another attempt to bring the island to the true faith was made from Italy. It is usually said that the bishops of Rome had lost interest in the English mission, which had hung fire for so many long years; and Gregory's successors certainly had not any great love for Gregory's schemes. It is very true that the work of the mission had hung fire; it had done nothing in the way of progress for a long time. Nay, its work had grievously shrunk; for the two kingdoms, other than Kent, which it had for a time converted, were, when Birinus came to Wessex, entirely pagan.

At this conjuncture Pope Honorius, bearing the same name as the Archbishop of Canterbury, a fact which has led some writers into error, received a visit from a man of missionary spirit, Birinus. Birinus declared that he wished to preach in Britain, beyond the parts occupied by the English, parts in which no teacher had preceded him. Either this betokened a curious ignorance of the circumstances of those parts of Britain which were not occupied by the English, or Birinus had acquired from the Scotic monks on the continent some special knowledge of remote parts of North Britain, which it would be very useful to us to possess [1]. However that might be, Pope Honorius applauded his resolve, and told him to obtain consecration as bishop at Genoa, from Asterius the Arch-

---

[1] Pope Honorius knew something about the Scotic Church, for he wrote a letter to them about their observance of Easter (Bede, *H. E.* ii. 19). Bede does not suggest that he made any appeal to them on the ground of a supposed foundation of their Church by any of his predecessors.

bishop of Milan, who was then resident at Genoa[1]. Why he should not tell him to look to the Archbishop of Canterbury for consecration, is a question which raises interesting points. We are speaking of a time just about the date of the relapse of Northumbria into paganism, and Archbishop Honorius had in all probability, indeed we may say certainly, not as yet received the pall, which was sent to him from Rome on June 11, 634. This may possibly have been the reason for passing him over; but the pall meant less by far in those days than later. It is to be remembered that Archbishop Honorius had himself been consecrated by Paulinus years before Paulinus received his useless pall. From another point of view, it

---

[1] Bede says (ii. 19) by Asterius, Bishop of Genoa. But no names of bishops of Genoa appear to be known between Paschasius, in A.D. 440, and John I, who subscribed the decrees of the Roman Council under Agatho in 680. Asterius, a Roman by birth, became Bishop of Milan in 628. He died at Genoa in 637 or 638. The statement of Ughelli (*Italia Sacra*, ed. 1652, t. 4, p. 91) is a useful example of the growth of Papal claims. "Asterius consecrated Bennus" (i.e. Birinus) "bishop, by order of the Pope, who sent him as legate into Britain."

It is quite possible that Asterius acted as Bishop of Genoa, as well as Archbishop of Milan, so that Bede's statement may not have been a mere blunder.

may possibly have been the fact that Pope Honorius wished to keep this new mission, to persons other than the English, clear of the ecclesiastical arrangements made for the English race. To have consecrated him himself might have given too much importance to the new attempt, and would no doubt have caused difficulty at Canterbury. The difference in principle, between that course and advising him to be consecrated by Asterius, was great.

However that may have been, Birinus was consecrated by Asterius, with a roving commission as it would appear, and he came to England. If he landed at Richborough, or Reculver, or on the Isle of Thanet, or at Lymne, he did not report himself to Archbishop Honorius, so far as Bede's statement informs us. But it is much more probable that he landed at least as far west as the Isle of Wight; for Bede says that he first entered the nation of the Gewissæ, and that was the earlier name of the West Saxons. An examination of the maps shews that Porchester was the point from which a great road ran to Winchester, and that probably was his landing-place.

Porchester was the place at which the

tribe of the Gewissæ, to be known later as the West Saxons, had landed for the conquest of that part of Britain only about a hundred and twenty years before. It lay at the mouth of the one way through impassable forests which led to the open downs of Caer Gwent, our Winchester. It was one of the three great Roman fortresses that had guarded the southern coast of Britain, so long as the Roman armies held the land. For a hundred years after they left, the Britons continued to hold it against the piratical bands of Jutes and Saxons, and holding it they held the key to the interior. It was not till the years 514 and 519, that a sufficient force came by sea to drive the Britons out of the mighty Roman walls. Once past Porchester, the way to Caer Gwent was open to them. Parts of the walls of Porchester still remain, with the sea close by, and with an interesting Norman church within the circuit of the walls, placed close to the wall. The Normans were fond of placing their chief churches near the walls, when they used ancient walls, or built walls, for the protection of their settlements.

Birinus had come to find a pagan people beyond the limits of the English. Here he was, among the English, and he found he had no need to push through to distant parts of the island to find the material for his work. "All the people there were most pagan." "He thought it more useful to preach the Word to them, than to go in search of those to whom he had come to preach." It is important to notice that there is no hint that he thought it advisable to refer this complete change of plan to Rome; that is, he did not come under any commission from Rome which needed revision; nor had Asterius imposed geographical limits upon his exercise of episcopal functions in this island.

In the province of the pagan West Saxons, then, he preached the Gospel. The king was Cynegils, great nephew of Ceawlin (the direct ancestor of the queen), who had been from 560 to 593 such a scourge to the Britons in the west, and of Ceolwulf, who had fought impartially with all the races he could find. He taught the king the principles of the Christian faith; then, when he was duly prepared, he catechized him, and baptized him. It was the office of the chief sponsor to receive the newly-baptized Christian by giving him his hand as he emerged from the laver of regeneration. This office was performed by the most holy and most victorious King Oswald, of Northumbria. Here, in a striking form, we have the Northumbrian influence in the conversion of a great Saxon kingdom, eventually the greatest of all. Kent had already dwindled, and was to dwindle still more. In the conversion of Wessex we lay our hand upon the Christianising of the finally dominant kingdom. And while it was done by a bishop from Italy, it was done in disregard of the original mission from Rome. Not only were there no relations between Birinus and the Canterbury mission, on the shewing of Bede himself, but also the one home influence there was, in the conversion of Wessex, was that of the most devoted adherent of the Scotic Church. Modern times have suggested, further, that Birinus is, after all, the Irish name Byrne with the r duly rolled; and the late Bishop Forbes of Brechin claimed that Kilbirnie in Ayrshire was named from him. We are not in a position to say that he was not an Irishman by origin, but the suggestion is a mere guess.

Along with the king, his people too were washed clean in the fountain of baptism. Steps were immediately taken to establish the Church of the West Saxons. Oswald,

Bede tells us, played an important part in this arrangement. After acting as godfather to King Cynegils, he married the king's daughter. This is a curious evidence that the plea of spiritual kinship was not then held to be of the importance which it assumed later. Oswald actually married his son's daughter, his own granddaughter, in the language of spiritual affinity. Having become, in ordinary language, the king's son-in-law, Oswald, strange as it may sound, joined Cynegils in the donation to Birinus of a place for his episcopal seat. What could this joint gift of a site in Oxfordshire, by the Kings of Wessex and Northumbria, mean? Bede, who no doubt understood what he was writing about, and was beyond question at least as much alive to the seeming anomaly as we can possibly be, living as he did in the period of separate kingdoms, tells us clearly that the two kings, "both kings," gave the city of Dorcic to Bishop Birinus. In the absence of any hint as to the reason for this alliance in donation, we may perhaps suppose that the King of Northumbria had acquired on his marriage some dowry right in Dorchester, the Dorchester near Oxford, and that the son-in-law's participation was necessary to validate the donation. Bede's remark has, I think, a not inconsiderable importance from another point of view. The fact that a King of Northumbria was joined with the King of Wessex in this first endowment of the Church in Wessex, seems to shew fairly conclusively that the gift was a personal gift by the two kings. It could not be in any sense a gift corresponding to what we in parliamentary times call a parliamentary gift. Queen Victoria, the direct heir of Cynegils, and not the Houses of Parliament with the queen at their head, represents the Wessex side of the donation. It was a royal, not a state, gift. It is a curious problem, why did they place their central seat of Christianity so near to the very extremity of the kingdom. Dorchester is only a few miles south of Oxford, not far from the northern boundary of the Gewissæ or West Saxons and the southern boundary of their Anglian foes of Mercia. It lies on the north side of the chalk hills, and there was then no great road across the several head-waters that lay between it and Silchester. The only answer I can give is that the King of Wessex was looking to the future; that his alliance with the great king of the north had developed his political ambition; and that he intended to extend his kingdom so far northwards that Dorchester should in the end become a central place.

Here, then, Birinus settled himself as Bishop of the West Saxons. He built and dedicated churches, Bede tells us; won many people to the Lord by his pious labours; died (in 650), and was buried at Dorchester. Bishop Hædda, who succeeded him in 676, translated his body to the city of Venta, that is, Winchester, and buried him there in the Church of the Blessed Apostles, Peter and Paul. I have had more than once to remark that Cardinal Vaughan, and all the Roman bishops in England, in claiming England as dedicated to St. Peter, put forth a solemn statement a year or two ago to the effect that the second church in Canterbury was dedicated to St. Peter, whereas the dedication was to St. Peter and St. Paul. In the same document they made the same statement with regard to Winchester, with the same absence of accordance with the well-known fact stated by Bede. It is true that in the Anglo-Saxon Chronicle there is the statement, under the year 644, that "Cenwahl ordered the old church at Winchester be built in St. Peter's name"; and, under the year 648, that "the minster which Cenwahl king caused make at

Winchester was builded and hallowed in St. Peter's name". But these are late additions. The phrase "the *old* church" shews that the addition of the word "old" was made after the year 900; for the "new minster" was only begun in the tenth century, and the two mentions of St. Peter are found first in a manuscript of the twelfth century. The earliest manuscript of all, our Cambridge MS., which was written in one hand down to the year 891, has none of these three insertions. This gives an awkward colour to the evidence for the dedication to St. Peter alone, if there was intention in it; but it is probably a sufficient explanation that the name was cut short to "St. Peter", as Bede sometimes cuts short the name of "St. Peter and St. Paul" at Canterbury. Bede was perfectly right, and the evidence of the charters leaves no question about it. A charter of 672 describes the church as "dedicated in honour of St. Peter, the chief of the apostles, and to St. Paul"; a charter of 737, "Peter and Paul"; a charter of 749, "Peter and Paul"; later in the century, "in honour of the blessed Trinity and the true Unity, and of the Apostles Peter and Paul." In 904 the phrase occurs, "the Monastery of the Church of

St. Peter;" it is singularly interesting to find this first mention of St. Peter alone only thirteen years after the truthful hand of the writer of the Chronicle had ceased from its labours. In 909 we find the new dedication, but still retaining the old, "to the reverend Trinity, and the blessed chief of the apostles and his co-apostle Paul[1]." Henry VIII. ordered that it should be called the Church of the Holy Trinity. In the restoration of the great screen of the Cathedral Church of Winchester by the late dean, Dr. Kitchin, the proper patron saints are represented by statues, St. Peter and St. Paul.

Not the Church of Winchester only, but the Church of Dorchester itself, the original bishop's seat, was dedicated to St. Peter and St. Paul. Indeed, so inseparable were these two saints, "the Princes of the Apostles," in the early Church, sharing as they did one great Saint's Day, that a dedication to one of them alone was relatively unusual. From a paper in the last issue of the St. Paul's Ecclesiological Society (III. v., Decem-

---

[1] These facts are provided for me by the Dean of Winchester. The references are, *Cartularium Saxonicum* (Birch), I. 46, 228, 257, 554; II. 78, 260, 302. See also p. 177.

ber, 1895), on Churches in West Kent, it appears that of 104 churches, sixteen were dedicated to St. Peter and St. Paul, one to St. Peter, one to St. Peter ad Vincula, and one to St. Peter and St. John Baptist. In the highly important document which Pope Vitalian sent to King Oswy on the death of Wighard, Archbishop elect of Canterbury, the pope associates St. Peter and St. Paul as the joint source of the true traditions; and he tells Oswy that Wighard had been buried at the threshold of the apostles. The "Apostolic See" was the See of the Apostles, not of the Apostle. It is a curious and interesting fact that the most Petrine of all English dedications, that which changed the name of Medeshamsted to *Petri Burgus*, Peterborough, was in fact not a dedication to St. Peter alone. Under the year 657, the Anglo-Saxon Chronicle, giving an exceedingly lengthy account of the whole proceedings, says that the monastery was hallowed in the names of St. Peter, St. Paul, and St. Andrew.

King Cynegils died seven years before Birinus, and was succeeded by his son Coinwalch. This man refused to receive the faith and the sacraments of the heavenly kingdom, and before long he lost his earthly kingdom. His wife was a sister of the powerful pagan Penda, King of the Mercians; that Penda, who on more than one occasion wrought such ruin in Northumbria, in concert with the Christian Britons, and eventually allowed his son to introduce Christian teachers into Mercia. Coinwalch put away Penda's sister, and took another wife. Penda was not at all a man to stand that sort of thing; he declared war, and drove Coinwalch from his kingdom. Coinwalch took refuge with the King of the East Angles, Anna, whom Penda eventually slew, as he had slain his Christian predecessors Ecgric and Sigebert. Anna was a most devoted Christian, as we shall see when we come to speak of East Anglia. Such a man did not leave his guest's paganism unassailed; and in three years' time Coinwalch became a Christian. Not long after, he was restored to his kingdom. What had been the state of Wessex in the interval, and what Birinus had been doing, Bede does not tell us.

The king, then, came back. After a time, he lost his bishop by death, as we have seen; and he wished to have another. Whence was this wish to be supplied? It was no very far cry to Canterbury, where Honorius was still archbishop; and the roads were good enough from the northern part of his realm. The Englishman Ithamar was bishop at Rochester, and there was in East Anglia, to which kingdom Coinwalch owed so much, a bishop in connection with Canterbury. Those were all the bishops of the Italian connection then in England; that is, in the year 650. In Northumbria, the first of the Scotic Bishops of Lindisfarne, Aidan, was still alive, being succeeded in the next year by Finan, who three years later restored our East Saxon bishopric by consecrating Cedd. It was from the Scotic Church that the second line of Bishops of Wessex came. "A certain pontiff from Hibernia," Bede tells us, "came into the province; associated himself with the king, and voluntarily undertook the ministry of preaching." His name was Agilbert. He was by nation a Gaul, of Paris, and he had spent no small time in Ireland for the purpose of studying the Scriptures. The fame of the Irish schools of learning was at that time great, and many persons went from Gaul to study there; a good many English too, especially later on in the century. Lismore was probably the principal of the Irish schools for the purposes of foreigners; but the interesting epitaphs still remaining there do not go so far back as

Agilbert's time by about 200 years[1]. Being in Waterford, Lismore was accessible for persons crossing from Britain. Tradition tells us that Aldfrith of Northumbria, who succeeded Ecgfrith in 685, and passed his youth in Ireland, was educated in Lismore. If Agilbert was there between 640 and 650, as seems probable, he would just miss the founder of the school, St. Carthach, who was banished from Rahin (Rathain) in 631, and died at Lismore in 636. At Rahin he had 710 students attending his teaching. There is a famous verse describing the character of his lectures; and as his successor is credited with being equally eloquent, we can imagine the influence brought to bear upon Agilbert:

> Loveth Mochuda (i.e. Carthach) the piety.
> Wondrous every history of his histories.
> Before him had not shed any one
> Half that he shed of tears [2].

---

[1] Bendacht for an̄ Martan, *a blessing for the soul of Martin* (Abbat Martin, died 878); bendacht for anmain Colgen, *a blessing for the soul of Colgan* (Colgan, a famous ecclesiastic, died 850; or do Donnchad, *a prayer for Duncan* (Donnchad and his cousin O'Bric, monarch-elect of the Desi, were assassinated in the cathedral, 1034); Suibno m̄ conhuidir, *Sweeny the son of the pale hound* (this well-known scribe and anchorite, Abbat of Lismore, died 854).

[2] I have to thank my friend Dr. Norman Moore for this information and translation.

In 640, St. Cathaldus was master of the school. The other great schools open to Agilbert were Bangor and Clonmacnois. Probably there were students also, even at that early date, at Armagh and Clonard.

Coinwalch soon saw how learned and how industrious Agilbert was, and he begged him to accept the episcopal seat, and remain as pontiff to the West-Saxon race. Agilbert consented, and for some years the arrangement held. But, in the end, the king, who knew no language but Saxon, got quite weary of the barbarous talk of his bishop,—the disrespectful phrase is not mine,—and brought in another bishop, who spoke the same tongue as himself, one Wini, consecrated in Gaul. He then proceeded to divide the province into two dioceses [1], placing Wini at Venta, that is, Winchester, and leaving Agilbert at Dorchester, shorn of the best parts of his diocese. Agilbert was very indignant that the king should have done this, without even consulting him. The proverb about half a loaf was perhaps not

---

[1] *Parochia*, parish, is of course Bede's word for "diocese." This has led to much confusion and misunderstanding as to the date of the division into parishes in the modern sense of the word.

current then. He left Wessex, and after some time returned to France, where he was made bishop of his native city, Paris, dying in that bishopric full of years. It was this Agilbert who played indirectly so large a part at the synod of Whitby, having gone from Wessex to live in Northumbria before his return to Gaul.

Wini's accession to Winchester is dated in 662, and on Agilbert's departure he probably exercised supervision over the whole province, though it is to be noted that Bede still calls Agilbert bishop of the West Saxons at the time of the synod of Whitby in 664. Coinwalch did not find bishops very easy people to get on with, and he very soon got rid of Wini, who took refuge with Wulfhere, king of the Mercians, over-lord of the East Saxons then. The "see of the city of London," as Bede here calls it, was vacant by the death of Cedd, and Wini bought it of Wulfhere; and bishop of London he remained for thirteen years, even to the end of his life, as Bede expressly says[1]. Meanwhile Coinwalch did without a bishop at all for several years, probably eight or not far short of that,

---

[1] See some remarks on this point on pages 120, &c.

till things began to go wrong with him. His enemies gave him great trouble and prevailed against him. At last he began to remember that when he disbelieved, in earlier years, he lost his kingdom; when he believed, he was restored. A sort of rule-of-three sum suggested that as he got on badly without a bishop, he might get on well if he appointed one. Thereupon he sent to France and begged Agilbert to come back. Agilbert replied that he was now bishop of his native city and diocese, and therefore he could not come. But he had a nephew—nepotism is derived from *nepos* a nephew—the priest Eleutherius[1], and he thought him worthy of the bishopric. The king accepted the suggestion and sent for Eleutherius. This was in 670, and by that time Theodore of Canterbury had already done a good deal towards unity of organisation with Canterbury as a centre. Coinwalch applied to Theodore to consecrate his bishop, and Theodore consecrated him. Thus of the first four bishops of Wessex, the only Englishman was the simoniacal Wini. The two-fold arrangement of dioceses seems to have dropped with Agilbert's retirement. His successor

---

[1] Or, Leutherius

Wini was sole bishop, at Winchester. Eleutherius was sole bishop, at Dorchester. Hædda moved the see to Winchester.

It is not necessary to point out that in all this story of Coinwalch's proceedings, we see no hint of anything but autocratic appointment of bishops and arrangement of sees by the king. Those who seek for arguments in favour of free election of bishops to places of great power by presbyters, or by clergy and laity, or by whatever other means are suggested in these days, had better look elsewhere than in early Wessex, or, indeed, than in English history at all.

Nor will those who seek here for early evidence of the sway of Rome in England fare any better. Coinwalch and Agilbert and Wini behaved as though they had never even heard the name of Rome. They might perhaps have behaved better, if they had shewn a sense of union and communion with the patriarch of the west; and if the patriarch of the west had imagined that it was at all his business, he might perhaps have kept them in better order. That does not touch the historical fact that Rome's hand was not felt in Wessex,—indeed was not stretched out.

The Isle of Wight had been conquered by

the West Saxons not long after their successful attempt on Porchester and their sack of Venta, our Winchester. Cut off from further conquests north and west of Winchester by the strong defence of the Britons, they spent the years before their great advance in the subjection of the island off the coast. It was won in 630. They did not occupy it themselves, but let it fall to the possession of their allies the Jutes. Later on, it was held with Wessex; till Wulfhere, the Mercian king, over-lord of Wessex, gave it to the South Saxon King on his conversion to the Christian faith. When we come to speak of Sussex we shall see how late that was, as late as the year 680. Soon after that, Ceadwalla, an exiled member of the house of Cerdic, seized the kingdom of Wessex, and won back the Isle of Wight from Sussex. It was at that time, so late as 686, wholly given to idolatry, and Ceadwalla endeavoured to put an end to this by destroying all the inhabitants and putting subjects of his own in their place. He had vowed that if he conquered the island he would devote a fourth part of it, and a fourth part of the spoil, to the Lord. This he performed by handing over a fourth part of the land to Wilfrith of

Northumbria, who, as we shall see when we speak of Sussex, happened to be working among the South Saxons then. According to the English manner of computation, the whole island was a land of 1,200 families, and Wilfrith received in possession a territory of 300 families. He set his sister's son Bernwin to do the work of Christianising the island, giving him as colleague the priest Hiddila.

The Isle of Wight does not geographically belong in whole to either of the two English kingdoms, Wessex and Sussex. As Bede points out, it lies opposite the division between the two. Thus it was counted now as part of one, now of the other kingdom, and its ecclesiastical position was uncertain. It never had a bishop of its own, nor, in Bede's belief, was it definitely under the rule of any bishop till Bede's own time, when it was placed under the jurisdiction of Daniel, bishop of the West Saxons. To the diocese of Winchester it still belongs.

The descent of the see of Winchester from the earliest times to the Reformation has been accompanied by several complications. To mention them will be the simplest way of shewing the gradual growth of the area of

Christian Wessex, and of its ecclesiastical arrangement.

First of all, as we have seen, it was placed at Dorchester, near Oxford. This fact the early Anglo-Saxon lists disregard. The lists they give are lists of Bishops of the West Saxons, as the London lists are Bishops of the East Saxons. These lists are found chiefly in the Anglo-Saxon MSS. presented by Archbishop Parker to his College, Corpus Christi, Cambridge. They are principally three, one being written late in the tenth century, the others about three quarters of a century earlier. From them we learn that on the death of Hædda, the fifth bishop, counting Birinus of Dorchester as the first, the West Saxon see was divided into two parochiæ or parishes, dioceses as we call them, Winchester and Sherborn. This indicates an extension of the kingdom south-westwards, after some hard fighting, and a change of view as to the expansion northwards. Daniel was made Bishop of Winchester, and Aldhelm Bishop of Sherborn, in 705.

It was this Aldhelm who brought from Lombardy a beautiful altar of white marble, adorned with sculptured crosses. And his chasuble was so beautiful that it was preserved as a work of early art at Malmesbury after the Conquest: its ornaments were peacocks in circles.

The opportunity of this division of labour was taken to place the Isle of Wight under Daniel's charge, in Bede's time.

Then, just before the earlier lists were compiled, the diocese of Winchester was itself sub-divided into parishes or dioceses, in 909. Frithestan—whose splendid stole and maniple are now at Durham, with an inscription formed of worsted-work letters inserted in the texture of woven gold thread, Queen "Ælflæd caused to be made for the pious Bishop Friðestan"—he held Winchester, and Athelstan held Ramsbury. This indicates a movement northwards, Wessex making itself sure of Berkshire as included in its episcopal oversight. It might be asked why it should not have resumed the seat at the northern Dorchester, the first home of its bishop. The answer is that Dorchester had then for some considerable time been reckoned to Mercia, and was held jointly with Lichfield[1].

At this same time, probably later in the

---

[1] See Lecture IV, pp. 125, 126.

same year, the sees of Wells and Crediton were established, not by sub-division, but by acquisition of territory, shewing great expansion to the west and north-west.

Thus we have in the early tenth century the Wessex sees of Winchester, Sherborn, Ramsbury, Wells, and Crediton. At the Norman Conquest they were all in existence. The bishop of Crediton, Leofric, had moved to Exeter in 1049, and he died in 1072; Osbern, the next bishop, was bishop of Exeter. Giso of Wells died in 1088, and his successor John of Tours was bishop of Bath and Wells. It so chanced that the see of Sherborn, which had lasted three hundred and seventy years, and the see of Ramsbury, which had lasted a hundred and seventy years, were held at the Conquest by one and the same man, Herman, and he made his home at Old Sarum. Old Sarum was in the course of time deserted for Salisbury.

Finally, in 1542, Bristol was erected into a bishopric, and in 1836 it was combined with a see of Mercian descent, Gloucester. Thus the original see of the West Saxons has by degrees grown into the sees of Winchester, Bath and Wells, Exeter, Salisbury, and half of Gloucester and Bristol.

Birinus and Cynegils and Coinwalch will appear in our transept windows among the primary bishops and primary Christian kings of the English Heptarchy.

LECTURE III.

EAST ANGLIA

Redwald.—Eorpwald.—Sigebert and Felix.—Dunwich and Elmham.—Schools of East Anglia.—Sigebert's death.—King Anna and his daughters.—Fursey.—Connection with Canterbury.—Dying out of the Augustinian succession.—Consecrations of bishops, 597-668.—Descent of the East Anglian see.

The kingdom of East Anglia corresponded in extent with our Norfolk and Suffolk, with at least that part of Cambridgeshire which lies to the east of the great Dyke (the Devil's Dyke) at Newmarket, and probably in early times more than that. The parishes in this corner of Cambridgeshire were in the East Anglian diocese till fifty or sixty years ago, when the archdeaconry of Sudbury was transferred to the see of Ely; one among many ecclesiastical arrangements which have served to obliterate old and interesting landmarks. The fen country up to Peterborough was probably reckoned with East Anglia at some periods of time, forming a principality of Fen-men which would count with Mercia or with East Anglia according to the political circumstances of the time.

Ethelbert, the King of Kent, was over-lord of the East Angles, as he was of the East Saxons, and indeed of all the English south of the Humber according to Bede. Bede tells us that he was the third who held this position. The first was Ælla, King of the South Saxons, about 490 A.D., a kingdom of which we hear so little after that; the next was Ceawlin of the West Saxons, about 560; then Ethelbert of Kent, the first Christian over-lord; and then Redwald, of the East Angles, of whom we are to speak to-day. The fifth, sixth, and seventh holders of this curious and ill-defined supremacy were the three successive Kings of Northumbria, Edwin, Oswald, and Oswy, all of whom added to their rule as Kings of the North a general supremacy as over-lords of the rest of England.

We saw last year how very important a part Redwald, King of the East Angles, played in the history of Northumbria. Edwin, the fugitive owner of the throne of Deira, was followed to his various places of refuge by the vindictive determination of Ethelfrith his brother-in-law, the rightful King of Bernicia, the usurping King of Deira. Edwin finally took refuge at the court of Redwald, King of the East Angles, probably at Rendlesham in Suffolk, a little to the north-east of Woodbridge. Exning was a royal seat somewhat later than this, but I do not know that we have any knowledge of it before Anna's time. Framlingham has been said, on less authority, to have been an early royal residence of the East Anglian kings. Ethelfrith sent messengers to Redwald, with great promises of money if he would put Edwin to death. A second and a third time he sent, increasing his promises and threatening war. Redwald, in fear of Ethelfrith, agreed either to kill Edwin or to deliver him up to the third messengers. But, suddenly, other counsels prevailed. He sent a third refusal, and like a wise man he backed it up with an army, so promptly that Ethelfrith had no time to make preparations, and was killed in battle on the banks of the Idle, probably near Retford, in 617. Redwald lost a son in the battle, and this loss increased the strength of the bond of gratitude which bound Edwin thenceforward to him. The result of the battle was that Edwin recovered his kingdom of Deira, and ruled also over the other portion of Northumbria, Bernicia.

When Edwin became a Christian, he felt that he must do what he could to repay the debt he owed to the King of the East Angles. Redwald, indeed, was dead, had died in 617, after some years—we do not know how many, I believe—of powerful rule and supremacy. His son Eorpwald had been reigning at least ten years in his stead, but without the wider over-lordship, which had now fallen to Edwin, whom his father had saved. To Eorpwald Edwin now addressed his persuasions towards a change of faith.

Redwald's connection with Christianity had been a very curious one. It is a unique instance in our early records of the attempt to hold two opposing faiths at once, or at least to propitiate two opposing superhuman powers. At some early period of his reign, not otherwise defined by Bede, he had been made a Christian on a visit to Kent. We may perhaps assume that this was during Ethelbert's over-lordship. Whenever it was, it was the only case in which we have a hint of an endeavour on the part of the original Italian mission to touch the East Angle kingdom. When Redwald returned from

Kent a baptized Christian, his wife disapproved what he had done; and she and certain evil teachers seduced him from his allegiance to Christ, or, rather, from the sincerity of his faith. From that time to the day of his death he had in one and the same temple an altar for the Christian sacrifice, and a little altar for the victims offered to demons. Aldwulf, who became king of the East Angles in 663, and lived to Bede's time, used to say that the temple thus strangely furnished by his great-uncle remained to his time, and he had seen it as a boy. Such was the example set to Redwald's pagan son Eorpwald, who was now to come under the Christian influence of Edwin.

Edwin persuaded Eorpwald to abandon his idolatrous superstitions, and with his whole province to receive the faith and sacraments of Christ. As Paulinus had certainly been at the court of Redwald at the great crisis of Edwin's career, we may not unreasonably suppose that as Edwin's bishop he had something to do with this wholesale conversion. But nothing of the kind is suggested by Bede, or is in any way to be gathered from the history. Nor is Canterbury or its Archbishop Honorius in any way referred to. Bede assigns the whole merit to Edwin's personal action. All that we can say, in the endeavour to assign to the Italian mission some sort of share in this particular conversion of an English kingdom, is, that Edwin owed his Christianity to Canterbury, and East Anglia owed its Christianity to Edwin. Certainly no attempt is recorded on the part of Canterbury to set up a bishopric in East Anglia when the kingdom had become Christian, nor yet to restore Christianity when the kingdom became pagan again. It is a dominant feature of the work of the Italian mission, that they were not dogged. They were fair-weather people, successful in time of success, nowhere in time of failure.

Eorpwald was slain by a pagan, Richbert, not long after his conversion[1], and for three years the kingdom was in relapse. Then a happy change came. Eorpwald's brother Sigebert, so Bede describes him[2], obtained the kingdom. This Sigebert was "in all ways

---

[1] Bede does not give us any nearer indication of date than this. The Anglo-Saxon chronicle puts Eorpwald's baptism in the last year of Edwin, 632.

[2] Later authorities make him half-brother, a stepson of Redwald, which seems a curious relationship to have led to succession to the throne.

a most Christian and most learned man." That is the concise panegyric of Bede. He had been exiled in Gaul during his brother's life—verily our early English ancestors were not remarkable for brotherly love—and there he had been admitted to the Christian Sacraments. These privileges he determined that his people should enjoy when he came to the throne. He got signal help from a bishop who came from Burgundy, Felix by name. Whether Sigebert and Felix had met in France—to use that name in its wider meaning, not incorrectly by the way, for the Franks had now conquered and annexed Burgundy—we do not know. It would seem natural to suppose that it was so, and that on this account Felix came to England; and from its naturalness it has been asserted to have been the fact. But all that Bede or any primary authority tells us is, that Felix "came to Honorius the Archbishop and shewed him his desire"—what the desire was we are not told—"and Honorius sent him to preach the Word to the aforesaid nation of the Angles." Dr. Hook adds[1] that when Felix and Sigebert determined to estab-

---

[1] *Lives of the Archbishops of Canterbury*, i. 113 (1st. ed.).

lish a bishopric, Felix applied to Honorius for consecration; and this is the usual statement. But Bede says nothing of the kind. On the contrary, he says that Felix was born and ordained in Burgundy; and "ordained" is the word which Bede uses to indicate the consecration of a bishop; as, for instance, "Augustine went to Arles and was ordained Archbishop for the English race [1]," "Augustine while still living had ordained Laurentius to the episcopate [2]." There is an interesting variation in usage in the case of Archbishop Honorius himself, of whom Bede remarks that Paulinus "consecrated" him bishop, in place of Justus of Canterbury, in the new stone church at Lincoln [3]; this was curiously enough six years before a pall was sent to Paulinus [4]. It must be remarked that Dr. Stubbs, the Bishop of Oxford, included in his *Registrum Sacrum Anglicanum* (Oxford, 1858) a consecration of Felix in 630, to the see of Dunwich, by Honorius of Canterbury, giving as the authority for the statement "Bede ii. 15." I have quoted above the

---

[1] *H.E.* i. 27. [2] *H.E.* ii. 4. [3] *H.E.* ii. 16.
[4] In ii. 18, Bede uses both "ordained" and "consecrated" in one sentence, in speaking of this consecration.

words[1] of Bede, and they do not appear to justify this use of them. But I know better than to treat with any lightness an opinion of Dr. Stubbs.

Felix had great success, "in accordance with the sacrament of his name," as Bede says: a very unusual and very interesting application of the word sacrament, forecasting the answer in our Catechism. The name Felix, happy, was the outward visible sign of the inward spiritual grace which marked and blessed his life's work. Bede, playing again upon the name, tells us that Felix brought the pagans out of their long subjugation to wickedness and unhappiness, and led them on to faith, and the works of righteousness, and the rewards of perpetual felicity.

Felix, then, became Bishop of East Anglia, and his episcopal see was set at the city of Dommoc, that is, Dunwich. Dunwich was the Roman Sitomagus, one of the few Roman places in East Anglia, and the only one close upon the sea. Here Sigebert constructed a palace for himself and a church for his bishop, using no doubt the Roman walls as

---

[1] The Latin words are as follows :—"Cujus (sc. Sigeberti) studiis gloriosissime favit Felix episcopus, qui de Burgundiorum partibus, ubi ortus et ordinatus est," etc.

a quarry, as the fate of Roman walls has been from that time almost to this. Dunwich long remained an important English city, with a considerable number of churches and important buildings. It is now of the nature of a village, with one church and the ruins of another. The Roman and Saxon ruins are in the sea, which has been encroaching there for at least twelve centuries. The old harbour was swallowed up in Edward III's time, when four hundred houses were swept away; between 1535 and 1600 four churches were swept away; and in 1677 the sea entered upon the market-place.

The date usually given for the foundation of the see of Dunwich is 630. This flies in the face of the Anglo-Saxon Chronicle (636); and it is difficult on other grounds, throwing us very early in Edwin's Christianity for his conversion of Eorpwald. In 673, in the time of the fourth bishop, Theodore's principle of multiplying bishoprics by sub-division of dioceses was put in operation in East Anglia, and a second see was set up, at Elmham. There are in East Anglia two Elmhams, North Elmham and South Elmham. The former lies in Norfolk, north of East Dereham. The latter is the name of a group of several villages in Suffolk, about the middle of the triangle formed by Harleston, Halesworth, and Bungay. As far as we can judge from the probabilities of the case, Dunwich would be retained as the see of the South Folk, and Elmham would be the see of the North Folk. This consideration would place the see at North Elmham, not at South Elmham. There are at North Elmham indications of former importance, a mound, and fosse, and remains of ancient walls; the palace, or manor house, was built in a corner of a camp. And an early East Anglian princess, daughter of the next king and sister of Etheldreda of Ely, lived and was buried at Dereham, close by, and her well is there now [1]. The place and neighbourhood were

[1] This was Witberga, daughter of King Anna. The theft of this lady's body from Dereham by the monks of Ely is recounted in the Ely MS., and may be found in the story of "The Camp of Refuge." In 907, King Edgar gave to Ethelwold, Bishop of Winchester, the minsters which heathen men had broken down, and he set to work to repair the minster of Ely, placing as abbat there the Prior of Winchester, Brithnoth. The king gave to the abbey the town of Dereham, with its treasured relics of Witberga; but the monks dared not carry off the body openly, and they had recourse to monastic methods in the year 974.

The Rev. H. L. Arnold, Vicar of Dereham, has kindly sent me the information in his possession in relation clearly of considerable importance in early times. But at South Elmham there are much more remarkable remains. A space of three and a half acres, called the minster yard, is enclosed within a bank and moat, and contains the ruins of a great church— great in the early times—externally 100 feet long, known as the Old Minster, with a square narthex, a nave, and an apse; as interesting a fragment of pre-conquest ecclesiastical building as you can well find. It is very near one of the Flixtons, which take their name from Felix. The Bishops of Norwich retained an episcopal residence at South Elmham down to the time of Henry VIII. South Elmham Hall is said to be built on the site of Bishop Herbert's palace (1091–1121), and even to contain part of the

to Witberga. The inscription on Witberga's well is as follows:—
"The ruins of a tomb which contained the remains of "Witberga, youngest daughter of Annas, King of the "East Angles, who died A.D. 654. The abbot and monks "of Ely stole this precious relic, and removed it to Ely "Cathedral, where it was interred near her three royal "sisters, A.D. 974."
It was not heathen men only that broke down minsters (monasteries). Under the year 1070 the Anglo-Saxon Chronicle has a very sweeping entry, "In Lent the king let harry all the mynstres that in Engle land were."

original building[1]. The villages round about are known as the South Elmhams, each going by the name of its dedication Saint; and this of course points to an ecclesiastical centre of much importance at South Elmham. But it is, I think, decidedly too near Dunwich to have been the seat of the second bishopric, and I regretfully give it up, and accept North Elmham as the other see. To South Elmham we may at least assign the dignity of having been the principal ecclesiastical development of the South Folk, rising in importance as church work made its way from Dunwich inland, and as the incursions of the sea and of the Danes threatened the coast more and more. Indeed it may well have become the ecclesiastical centre in place of Dunwich; and in that case both North

---

[1] This information I owe to the Rev. E. McClure, who gives me also the internal lengths of the three parts of the church,—narthex (square) 26 ft., nave 37 ft., apse 22 ft. The figures for the length and breadth of narthex and nave look like multiples of 13 ft. Biscop's church at Wearmouth was arranged in multiples of 11 ft. Mr. McClure has found that there is no mention of this Old Minster in Domesday, or in the *Taxatio* of Pope Nicolas, and suggests that it was already a ruin at the time of the Conquest. The entrance at the west is by one central door; from the narthex to the nave there are two doors, towards the north and south.

Elmham and South Elmham may have been the seats of bishops of East Anglia, one for the North Folk and the other for the South Folk.

As we have seen, Bede describes Sigebert of East Anglia as very learned. He determined that others should be learned too. During his residence in France he had seen the care bestowed upon schools there, and when he came to his throne, he set himself to work to establish similar schools in East Anglia. He set up a school in which the youth might be instructed in letters. Felix, whom in this place Bede says Sigebert had received from Kent, gave him valuable assistance, and provided him with pedagogues and masters after the manner of the Kentish people. I do not remember that up to this time we have been told of the existence of schools of this kind in Kent. Thirty years later, or more than that, Theodore and Hadrian established the famous school of Canterbury; but we gather from Bede that it was then something new.

Bede does not say that Felix got the masters from Kent. It is quite possible that he got them from his home in Burgundy. In that case England richly repaid the debt when Alcuin sent to Charlemagne some of his pupils from the great school of York, "scions of paradise," as he rather enthusiastically described the scholars of the Cathedral School; and still more when he went himself to France and became Charlemagne's right-hand man in all that related to education and erudition.

In the Commemoration of Benefactors in the University of Cambridge, we used to trace our origin to this Sigebert of East Anglia. We declared that it had been handed down in history that first of all Sigebert, King of the East Angles, established a school of learning in Cambridge, and it was fostered and enlarged by the liberality of succeeding kings. This had the happy effect of making us about 240 years older than the University of Oxford, which in a very similar manner claims to have been founded by King Alfred. But now that the historic sense—or conscience—has become more learned and more acute, we in Cambridge at least have modified our statement, confining ourselves to the fact that Sigebert did set up in our part of the world a school or schools of learning. Geographically, it has been said that Cambridge or Grantchester was at that time in Mercia, not in East Anglia at all. But Bede says clearly that Ely was in East Anglia¹, and that when it was desired to find a coffin that would serve for the resting-place of the body of Etheldreda, the daughter of Sigebert's cousin and successor, the monks rowed up the water to Grantchester² and found there a sarcophagus of white marble, which they carried in their boat to Ely. We may fairly claim that Cambridge was then in East Anglia.

Sigebert had during this time had a sub-king under him, his kinsman Ecgric ruling a part of his kingdom. How the land was subdivided I think we do not know; but it is reasonable to suppose that the parts which we call Norfolk and Suffolk were the main kingdom, and the province of the Gyrvii was the other part, including Ely and Peterborough³. The scorn of the "folk" for the people of the "sheers" (shires) may conceivably be a relic of this division.

After a few years' experience of the labours of a king, Sigebert determined to retire, and leave Ecgric to rule the whole. He had built

---

¹ *H.E.* iv. 19.

² *Ibid.*: "a deserted city of small size." This is of course a powerful argument against the claim of Cambridge to be the site of one of Sigebert's schools.

³ *Ibid.* iv. 6. Bede says that Medeshamsted was in the region of the Gyrvii.

for himself a monastery, and here he now went to live, receiving the tonsure. But he was not allowed to end his days in peace. The pagan Penda, ubiquitous in mischief, invaded East Anglia. The leaders found themselves unable to cope with his forces; and so great was their belief in Sigebert's skill and influence, that they brought him, against his will, out of his monastery, and set him to lead them against the enemy. They felt sure, we are told, that the people would not dare to run away in his presence. Sigebert refused to be armed, and went into battle with a wand in his hand. He and Ecgric were killed, and the East Anglian army was destroyed. That was the end of this most Christian and most learned king.

Anna, the next king, a first cousin of Sigebert, was quite as remarkable for Christian graces as Sigebert had been, and his family of daughters made a mark upon the Christian work and history of England and of France. He was himself killed in 654 by that same Penda who had slain his two predecessors. Near Blythburgh in Suffolk is a district called Bulcamp Forest, and local tradition makes that the scene of the defeat and slaughter of Anna. The story is probably correct that Anna was buried at Blythburgh; but the tomb shewn there as his is in fact the tomb of Sir John Swillington. Anna it was who provided Coinwalch, King of Wessex, with an asylum, when Penda of Mercia drove him from his kingdom. As we saw two days ago, he took this favourable opportunity of converting Coinwalch to Christianity, being, as Bede says[1], "a good man, happy in a good and pious offspring;" and in another place he says of him[2], "a man truly religious, in all ways remarkable in mind and work." His brother Ethelhere succeeded him, the husband of St. Hilda's sister. It would appear that Penda allowed him to reign, and used him as a pretext—on what ground we do not know—for an invasion of Northumbria, requiring his armed assistance against King Oswy. Ethelhere and Penda were both of them killed in this expedition; and Aldwulf, of whom we have already spoken, Hilda's nephew, succeeded. We need not pursue the history of East Anglia further.

The early Christianity of East Anglia, and the reign of Anna, were marked by two features on which Bede dwells at unusual length. The one was, the dedication of so

[1] *H.E.* iii. 7.   [2] *H.E.* iv. 19.

many of Anna's daughters to the religious life; the other was the presence in East Anglia of the Irish hermit Fursey.

The oldest of Anna's daughters was Sexberga. She was wife of Earconbert, King of Kent, whom she married soon after 640. Two of her sons, Ecgbert and Hlothere, were kings of Kent; and Wulfhere of Mercia married one of her daughters. On her husband's death in 664, she founded the monastery of Minster, in the Isle of Sheppey, and thence went to her sister Etheldreda's abbey of Ely, where, in 679, she succeeded her sister as abbess. Her own daughter, Eormenhild, Wulfhere's widow, succeeded her as Abbess of Ely, and another daughter Werberga as Abbess of Sheppey. That brief sketch shews the wide influence of her life in those early days of the establishment of Christianity and the development of the religious life.

Etheldreda was in some respects the greatest of the daughters. She married, about 652, an East Anglian prince, Tonbert, who gave her Ely as a marriage gift. It was only nominally a marriage. On Tonbert's death she married in 660 Ecgfrith, Oswy's son, again a nominal marriage. He became King of Northumbria in 670, and about two years later the king let her go, and took a real wife. Her foundation of the Abbey of Ely is a familiar story.

The other daughters of Anna were Witberga, an Ely nun, of whom we spoke in connection with Dereham [1], and Ethelberga, a natural daughter, Bede says. Ethelberga introduces us to a noteworthy feature of those times, namely, the extent to which English ladies went to France to be educated [2] and made nuns. The principal schools for this purpose were the Monasteries of Brie, Chelles near Paris, and Andelys on the Seine. Ethelberga went to Brie, near Meaux, whose foundress Fara (hence the well-known name of the monastery, Faremoustier) was still living. So great were Ethelberga's virtues, that in the course of time she was made abbess. The same fortune had previously fallen to the lot of King Anna's step-daughter Sæthryd. It adds much to our interest in these ladies to know that Anna's brother and successor Ethelhere married Heruswith [3], St. Hilda's sister.

[1] See p. 78.
[2] See also *Lessons from Early English Church History*, S.P.C.K., p. 87.
[3] The writers of *Gallia Christiana* (viii. 1700) make both Sæthryd and Ethelberga daughters of Heruswith, and make Anna marry Heruswith and be the father of Ethelberga: they also say that a French writer had

The presence of the Irish Saint Fursey in East Anglia evidently stirred the interest of Bede. He came of the royal houses of Leinster and Munster, and after a long sojourn and marvellous visions on the shores of Lough Corrib, he came over to this island and made his way to "Saxony," that is, East Anglia. There he settled himself in the remains of the great Roman fortress of Cnobhersburg, whose massive walls, still fourteen feet high, and solid round towers fourteen feet in diameter, move the wonder of the present generation, much as Richborough and Pevensey do. The place is now called Burghcastle. It is near Lowestoft.

Here Fursey had a succession of visions such as he had had in Ireland. They closely resemble those of Drythelm, the Northumbrian, which I have described elsewhere in connection with the ornamentation of the stone church of Monkwearmouth, and the origin of the tradition that the north is the devil's side of a church [1]. To these visions the mediaeval

proved that "natural daughter" did not mean what in later times it meant. The ordinary statement as to Heruswith is that given in the text. The early Ely historian gives the same account as the writer in *Gallia Christiana*.

[1] *Lessons from Early English Church History*, S.P.C.K., p. 45.

details of the torturing of souls in the flames of hell are in great part due. Fursey left East Anglia when he realised that troublous times were in store for that land from the incursions of barbarians, and went to Gaul. There he left a mark which is still fresh, at Laon, Péronne, and St. Quentin, and other places in those parts, so well worthy of a sympathetic pilgrimage[1]. At Péronne his body remained fresh and uncorrupted in the time of William of Malmesbury. The face survived the horrors of the French Revolution, to suffer grievous things in the bombardment of Péronne by the Prussians in 1870. It was, however, saved from the fire, and is now a priceless relic in careful hands. The Curé of Péronne informs me that it was found under the ruins, with the glass of the reliquary melted by the action of the fire, and in its molten state taking the impression of the face[2]. From the connection between Fursey

[1] See a very charming book by Miss Margaret Stokes, *Three Months in the Forests of France*, George Bell & Sons, 1895.

[2] The Curé's account is sufficiently interesting to be reproduced here: "La face fut extraordinairement conservée au milieu de l'incendie occasionné par le bombardement prussien de 1870. Elle fut retrouvée au milieu des décombres de l'Eglise, recouverte de l'enveloppe en cristal de son reliquaire liquéfiée sous l'action du feu, et qui après l'avoir préservée en à conservé l'empreinte."

and Felix, it has been suggested in recent times, as a conjecture, that Felix himself may have been one of the colony of Irish monks assembled at Luxeuil in Burgundy. If that is so, he was, if the phrase may be allowed as congruous, a native of Ireland born in Burgundy [1].

East Anglia was the one English kingdom, other than Kent, which looked in its early days to Canterbury for the succession of its bishops. When Felix died, in 647, his deacon Thomas, of the province of the Gyrvii, that is, as I suppose, a subject of the sub-kingdom, was consecrated bishop in his place by Honorius of Canterbury; and when Thomas died, five years later, Honorius put in his place a Kentish man, Berhtgils, surnamed Boniface. This was the last appointment or consecration by Honorius, who died at a great age the year after, in 653.

Boniface occupies a highly important position, as being the last survivor of the bishops who traced their episcopal orders to Augustine. In him the Augustinian succession, never large, died completely out. He died in 669, and Deusdedit and Damian, his only companions in descent from Augustine, had

[1] See also p. 48.

died in 664. The facts are of sufficient interest to be set out in the form of a genealogical tree. If we count Felix as one of the succession, the Augustinian bishops number thirteen. *Sine prole* means that so far as history tells us, the bishop to whose name it is affixed did not consecrate any bishop; that is, that no one carried on an episcopal succession from him.

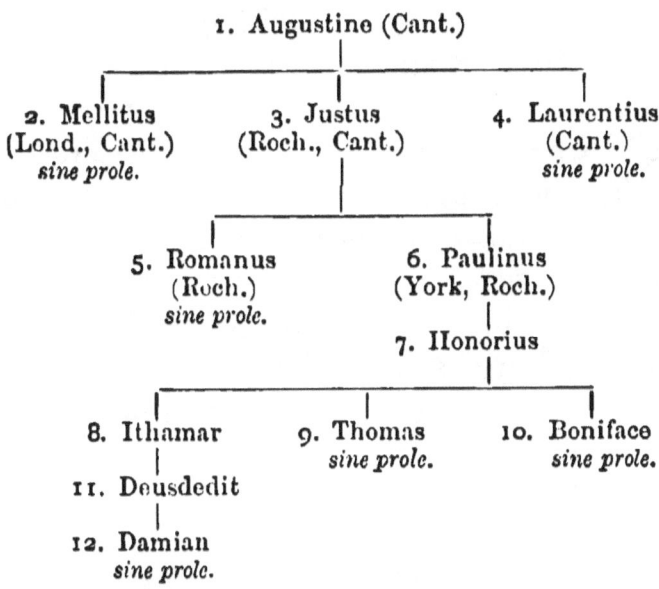

It may be added, for the facts are valuable as well as interesting, that from the coming of Augustine to the choosing of Theodore, that is, in the first seventy years of the existence of the Church of England, there were twenty-seven consecrations of bishops and archbishops who performed episcopal functions in the English kingdoms [1], whether consecrated specially for that purpose or not. Eleven of these consecrations were performed by Augustine or those who derived their episcopal orders from him; four were performed by "French" bishops; one by a Lombard bishop or archbishop; one by Wini, in "French" orders, and two British bishops; ten were performed by Scotic or Irish bishops. In this statement of numbers I have not reckoned Felix, who must be counted among the French or the Augustinian consecrations according to the view taken in regard to him. Among the Scotic consecrations I have reckoned the predecessor of Aidan. Arranged in kingdoms, the consecrations are as follows:—

	Augustinian	Other Sources
Kent	7	1
Northumbria	1	7
Wessex	0	3
East Anglia [1]	2	0
Mercia	0	4
East Saxons	1	1
Sussex	0	0
	11	16

From 655, when Deusdedit consecrated

[1] Not classing Felix.

Damian to Rochester, down to 668, when Pope Vitalian consecrated Theodore to Canterbury, not one of the nine consecrations was performed by any one connected with Augustine's mission.

Boniface was bishop for seventeen years, and after him Bisi was made bishop, Theodore consecrating him. Bisi was at the Synod of Hertford in 673, "a man of much sanctity and religion." He, again, is of special interest to us, because he is I think the first recorded instance of an English bishop permanently incapacitated by illness; and also because this illness led to the first mention I can remember of the election of an English bishop[1]. Bede says, "While he was still alive, but prevented from administering his bishopric by a very severe infirmity, Ecci and Badwini were *elected* and consecrated bishops in his place (or, to act for him[2]); whence that province is wont to have two bishops to this day." There is another instance of an infirm bishop, twenty years later, in the year 692, and it is a singularly interesting fact that

[1] Deusdedit, a West Saxon, not a Kentish man, was "elected" archbishop in 655, after a vacancy of eighteen months.

[2] *H. E.* iv. 5 "duo sunt pro illo electi et consecrati episcopi."

there again we have mention of the election of a substitute. "Bosel," Bede tells us, "the Bishop of the Province of the Wiccii"—our Worcestershire—"laboured under such infirmity of body that he could not perform his episcopal duties; wherefore, by the judgement of all, Oftfor was elected to the bishopric in his stead, and by the king's order was consecrated by Wilfrith, the Archbishop of Canterbury being dead and no successor as yet appointed." It may be noted that in describing the election of Oftfor, Bede remarks that for the vacancy which Bosel filled when he was made bishop, one Tatfrid had been elected, but he died before consecration. When Wilfrith was turned out of his Northumbrian see, those who filled his place are not described as "elected"; they were "substituted."

The bishopric of Dunwich came to an end with the incursion of the Danes. We have just the name of one successor to Wilred, the fifteenth bishop, whose last signature as bishop is found in 845, and then the see of Dunwich drops out of existence.

The newer see, Elmham, on the other hand, went on fairly steadily, in spite of the Danes. Stigand was bishop here in 1043, before he was moved to Winchester, and then to

Canterbury; it was he who crowned Harold, and after him Edgar the Atheling. Herfast, the first Norman bishop of East Anglia, removed the see from Elmham, and settled it at Thetford, about 1070. Thetford was a place of great importance from very early times. Its earthworks, formed of chalk, the natural soil, are perhaps the largest and most important in England, a double rampart, twenty feet high and 1000 feet in circumference, enclosing a mound 100 feet high. At the time of the Domesday Survey, when it was the seat of the East Anglian bishopric, thirteen churches are named; and the number rose to twenty. There are now three.

Finally, in 1091, or about that date, the third Norman bishop of East Anglia, Herbert de Losinga, who is said to have had a residence at South Elmham also, deserted Thetford and set his bishop's seat at Norwich. Here he laid the foundation[1] of the great

---

[1] It is pleasant to record that the Dean of Norwich is arranging a commemorative ceremony for the 800th anniversary of the foundation, on July 1, 1896. And it is very interesting to record that in the 800th year from the foundation of the cathedral church, a part of the shaft of the pre-Norman churchyard cross of St. Vedast's church has been found. It is the only piece of sculpture of this character known in East Anglia, so far as I am

Norman Cathedral in 1096. The work carried out in his time comprised the choir and its aisles, the tower, and the transepts. Thirteen years after the first stone was laid Ely was made a bishopric, taking parts of East Anglia and parts of Mercia. Peterborough, erected into a bishopric in 1541, completes the number of the sees which look in any sense towards an East Anglian origin [1].

We have had to consider at St. Paul's which of the kings, Redwald and Eorpwald and Sigebert, we shall place in our transept window among the primary Christian kings of the Heptarchy. Redwald's dual allegiance, to Christ and to demons, has cost him his place. Eorpwald scarcely lived to prove his Christianity as king, but he was the king of the first conversion. The honour falls to Sigebert of having been the king of the restoration. They will both appear. The representative of East Anglia among the twelve primary bishops is of course Felix.

---

aware. It is of the type of ornamentation found in Derby and other parts of the north occupied by Danes; and it is the earliest post-Roman relic Norwich possesses. It has been placed in the spacious Museum in the great Norman keep.

[1] See the statement in Bede, *H.E.* iv. 6, quoted in a note on p. 83.

LECTURE IV.

MERCIA

The name and the people.—Penda.—Marriage connections between Penda and Oswy.—Elfleda and Penda.—Baptism of Penda.—Death of Penda.—See of Lichfield.—Wulfhere.—Withdrawal of the Scotic Church.—Chad's consecration.—Development of the See of Mercia.—Offa and the Archbishopric of Lichfield.

THE great central kingdom of England, known as Mercia, seemed likely, at one time and another, to become the dominant kingdom. It did, as a matter of fact, occupy that position more than once. Nothing can well have seemed more unlikely, in the earlier times of the Heptarchy, than that Mercia and Northumbria would have to yield to Wessex. If you look at the maps of Britain in 658 and Britain in 665, in Green's *Making of England*, you will see in the former the enormous territory which recognised the supremacy of Oswy, at least five-sixths of the whole of England, and in the latter the absorption by Wulfhere of Mercia of nearly the whole of England south of the Humber.

Mercia, that is the march-land or borderland, is clearly not a name suitable for a great central territory. It was properly applied to the north-west part of the broad extent of country to which it eventually gave its name, the part where the West Angles marched with the Britons of North Wales and the Britons of Cumbria. In the times of which we are to speak, it appears from Bede that three subdivisions of the whole midland country were recognised, namely, the North Mercians, the Middle Angles, and the South Mercians[1]. The people throughout were Angles, not Saxons or Jutes. The territories of the North Mercians were larger than those of the South Mercians, from which they were separated by the river Trent, in the proportion of 7 to 5, the former being in Bede's phrase a land of 7,000 families, the latter of 5,000. This is his ordinary way of reckoning. Sussex, he tells us, was a land of 7,000 families, and the Isle of Wight of 1,200. A land of ten families appears to have been the usual amount for the endow-

---

[1] For the modern equivalents of Mercia see pp. 124, &c.

ment of a monastery. King Oswy founded twelve such[1], when he killed that Penda of whom we have so much to say to-day; and Hilda acquired a property of ten families for her famous Abbey of Whitby[2].

With the exception of Kent, whose conversion came first of all, and Sussex, whose conversion came last, it may be said generally that the kingdoms of the Heptarchy passed through the most critical periods of the establishment of Christianity in the course of the years between 633 and 655. Those were, as it happens, the limits of the reign of Penda, King of the Mercians, who lived and died a pagan. He was a determined enemy of his Christian contemporaries, whether Angles or Saxons; but when he found a powerful ally who was a Christian, he was quite willing to use his help against a common enemy. This was markedly the case in the great alliance between Penda and the Christian Britons under Cadwalla, when each desired to destroy the power of the Northumbrian Angles. If success against the enemy was to be taken as a sign of the favour and of the relative power of the gods and of

---

[1] Bede, *H. E.* iii. 24.   [2] *Ibid.*

the test which some of the Italian teachers of the English unwisely proposed, then Penda was indeed a favourite of the higher powers; and he may well have argued that paganism was superior in that respect to Christianity. He began his career by killing in a great battle Edwin, the first Christian king of Northumbria. Later on, he killed in another great battle the next Christian king of Northumbria, Oswald. He drove from his kingdom Coinwalch, the first Christian king of Wessex. He killed, in one battle, both the pious Sigebert of East Anglia, who had resigned his crown, and Ecgric the reigning king. In the next generation he killed Anna, who succeeded Ecgric in the kingdom of East Anglia. Five important kings killed in twenty-two years, all Christians, all like himself descended from Woden, and all Angles, was surely a very large measure of the highest kind of success for a pagan Anglian king. A sixth king, Ethelhere, of the East Angles, King Anna's brother, was killed in the battle in which Penda himself was killed; but he seems, strangely enough, to have been fighting on Penda's side.

Penda's first appearance on the pages of history was in this wise. Edwin of Northumbria, the first Christian king of the north of England, had come in the course of a long and successful reign to rule over the Britons in the west as well as over his own people on the east side of England. He was in some very real sense the over-lord of the Britons. Bede well understood the relations between the English and the Britons, who were very far from being extirpated or harmless even in his time [1], and he makes the fact of Edwin's sovereignty over the Britons quite clear. Cadwalla, the King of the Britons, rebelled against his over-lord, Edwin, and obtained the help of Penda, not then King

---

[1] To make this point clear—it is sometimes left obscure —Bede's summary of the relations between the English and the neighbouring peoples at the close of his history in A.D. 731, just a hundred years after Penda's beginning, is worth giving here (*H.E.* v. 23): "The nation of the "Picts is now under treaty of peace with the Anglian "race, and rejoices in being partaker with the universal "Church in Catholic peace and truth. The Scots [Irish "by race] who inhabit Britain are content with their "boundaries and have no hostility to the Anglian race. "The great majority of the Britons hate the Anglian "race, and wickedly oppose the appointed Easter of the "whole Catholic Church; but the power of God and of "man is too much for them, and they cannot have their "will in either respect; for while, in part, they are their "own masters, they are to some extent brought into "subjection to the Angles."

of Mercia, but of the Mercian royal race, and king from that year. Their united forces killed Edwin, and destroyed his army, in 633. One of Edwin's sons, Osfrid, was killed in the battle. Another, Eadfrid, gave himself up to Penda, and was by him slain some time after, contrary to his oath.

On this occasion it was Cadwalla, not Penda, that reaped the fruits of victory. Cadwalla it was who put to death the two young kings who were set up by the English to succeed Edwin; and Cadwalla, not Penda, ruled over Northumbria, till Oswald put an end to the British occupation and to Cadwalla's life.

But when next we find Penda operating against Northumbria, it is in his own name and on his own account. It was he who slew Oswald, in 642, and for many years grievously oppressed Oswald's successor Oswy. And here we come to the curious cross-relationships between Oswy's family and Penda's which are so puzzling. Edwin himself had married in his younger days a Mercian princess, Cuenburga, daughter of King Ceorl[1],

---

[1] Ceorl was the king usually called Creoda, or Crida, Penda's grandfather. Thus Penda was Edwin's nephew-in-law.

and she was the mother of his sons whom we have mentioned, Osric slain by Cadwalla and Eadfrid slain by Penda. His other children, Wuscfrea and Eanfleda, were by Ethelburga of Kent. Oswy married Eanfleda, the daughter of Edwin, who had been carried to Kent by Paulinus in his flight after Edwin's death. She was born in 627, and is supposed to have married Oswy about 651. But he, too, had been married before, and had at least two children before he married Eanfleda. Who his first wife was is not known; but it is surmised that she was of Penda's kin. His daughter Elfleda married Penda's son in 653, two years before the final war between the two nations in which Penda at last was killed. His son Alchfrith had some time before married Cyneberga, Penda's daughter, and as sub-king of Deira he gave his father Oswy much trouble, of what nature we are not told by Bede. The inscription on the Bewcastle cross[1] asks a prayer for the high sin of his soul, and this may have reference to the trouble of which Bede speaks. If it had been a question of apostasy, Bede would not have passed it over in silence. Alchfrith was on

---

[1] See Lecture VII, p. 203.

terms with his father when the Mercian crisis came in 655, for he fought on Oswy's side; and in 664 he and his father were together at the Synod of Whitby. I am inclined to think that after 664, between that date and 670, some offence was committed by the Catholic Alchfrith which Bede did not wish to mention, and in connection with which he lost his life. Certainly the inscription on the Bewcastle cross speaks of him in 670 as "once king," and concludes with bidding prayer for the high sin of his soul. That he was deeply Mercian in interests may be gathered from the fact that on the cross set up to his memory the names of the Mercian princess Cyneberga his wife, the Mercian king Wulfhere his brother-in-law, and the Mercian queen Cyneswitha, Wulfhere's wife, all appear. Cyneswitha held Oswy's other son Ecgfrith as a hostage at the time of the final battle in which Penda fell. If Ecgfrith was the son of Eanfleda, and thus only half-brother to Alchfrith, he can only have been a year or two old at the time, and that is not a very likely age for a hostage. On the other hand, that the hostage was in the queen's hands may not improbably point to a tender age. In any case, the fact of one of Oswy's two sons being a hostage shews how real the oppression by Penda was.

There are other curious indications of cross connections which it is difficult to understand. The son of the Most Christian King Oswald, Ethelwald, himself an exemplary Christian, the patron of Cedd and of Chad, was with Penda's army on the great occasion of Penda's last fight, in arms against his uncle Oswy. He did not, it is true, actually fight; he withdrew, Bede tells us, and awaited the result of the battle. Inasmuch as Ethelwald had been King of the Deiri, and, as we must understand, Alchfrith now held that position, it may have been that Oswy had turned out Ethelwald, who had in consequence gone over to Penda. And, quite inexplicably, Ethelhere, the Christian King of the East Angles, not only was fighting on Penda's side, but is described by Bede as the cause of the war. He was killed. It was his niece Etheldreda who married Oswy's son Ecgfrith, and on leaving him founded Ely.

This being premised, we can follow the course of the conversion of Mercia without being called off from time to time to look into political difficulties.

In or about the year 653, while the Italian

mission at Canterbury was slowly dying in the person of its latest representative Honorius, the first step in the conversion of Mercia was taken. Penda had a son Peada, whom Bede describes as "an excellent young man, completely worthy of the title and dignity of king." Penda promoted him to the sub-kingship of the Middle Angles, and he looked about for a queen. He came to Oswy, King of the Northumbrian Angles, and asked for his daughter Elfleda. The life in the *Acta Sanctorum* makes her the daughter of Eanfleda, that is, the grand-daughter of Edwin and Ethelberga, and great-grand-daughter of Ethelbert and Bertha, grand-daughter with six "greats" before it of Clovis and the Christian princess Clothilde, who won Clovis over to Christianity. That remarkable series of Christian princesses, in a line of eight descents from mother to daughter, whose pagan husbands became Christian kings, Clovis, Ethelbert, Edwin, Peada, almost tempts us to overlook the difficulty of dates in the last of the four cases. Eanfleda was born in or about 627, and was married somewhere about 651; her daughter cannot possibly have been marriageable in 653. All that we really know of the date of Eanfleda's marriage

is consistent with an earlier date than 651;
but it is at most a question of a year or two,
and she cannot have been Elfleda's mother.
We only know that her marriage was in
Aidan's lifetime; and we know it from
a very curious fact. The priest Utta, who
was held in high honour by princes and
people alike, and was abbat of the monastery
" at the goat's head," that is Gateshead, was
sent by Oswy to Kent, to bring his promised
bride Eanfleda. He asked Aidan's prayers for
the journey. Aidan told him they would
have a tremendous storm on the return
voyage, and gave him a vessel (*ampulla*)
of blessed oil, bidding him cast the oil upon
the waters when the crisis came. It all fell
out as Aidan said, and the oil stilled the
raging of the storm. Cynemund, a most
trustworthy priest of the church of Jarrow,
told Bede the story as Utta told it to him.
Inasmuch as our own generation has seen the
re-discovery of this method, and oil is now
regularly used as Utta used it, we can accept
the story even without Cynemund's testimony. Two years ago I gave another example
of this miracle of the oil upon the waters [1].

[1] *The Church in these Islands before Augustine*, S.P.C.K., p. 91.

Elfleda, then, was asked in marriage by Peada, probably her cousin. Her father Oswy and her brother Alchfrith claimed that Peada, if he was to marry her, must become a Christian, and bring to Christ the people over whom he ruled. Clearly Christianity had made very large strides since the time when all that the Frankish King of Paris, or whoever made the treaty for Bertha's marriage, could demand, was that the princess should be allowed to practise her religion; and since the time when all that Eadbald, the Christian king of Kent, could obtain, was that Edwin should allow Ethelberga the full exercise of her religion, and would himself become a Christian if on careful inquiry Christianity was found to be a better religion than his own.

Peada at once submitted to a course of instruction in the Christian faith. When he learned the promise of the heavenly kingdom, the hope of resurrection and of immortality in the world to come, he declared that he would gladly become a Christian, wife or no wife. The person who had most influence with him in this resolve was his brother-in-law Alchfrith, Oswy's son, who had married his sister Cyneburga.

By this time Aidan was dead, and it fell to the lot of Finan, the second Scotic bishop of Lindisfarne, to baptize the Mercian prince. The ceremony took place at the well-known royal residence called "At the Wall," that is, "on the Roman wall." This, as we know from another passage of Bede, lay twelve miles from the sea, and therefore was at or near Walbottle. My own opinion[1] is that Benwell may claim to be the representative of the place, meaning as it does "the head of the wall." Along with Peada, the whole of his companions and their dependants, military and domestic, were baptized, and Peada and they all went home rejoicing. Four priests were sent with him, such as for their learning and holiness of life seemed meet to teach and baptize the Middle Angles. They were Cedd, who afterwards came to us East Saxons; Adda, brother to Utta who stilled the waves with Aidan's blessed oil; and Betti; these three were Angles: and Diuma, a Scotic priest, of whom we shall hear again. I remarked last year on the wisdom and breadth of view shewn by the Scotic ecclesiastics in sending so large a

---

[1] See also p. 136.

proportion of Anglian teachers. They shewed a spirit very much the opposite of that with which the Celtic Christians are usually credited.

These four competent missionaries preached to the Middle Angles with great success. Every day the people came over to them, both nobles and those of lower degree, renounced the vileness of idolatry, and were washed clean in the fount of faith.

And, remarkably enough, it was not only among the Middle Angles of Peada's sub-kingdom that they preached. The murderous old pagan Penda allowed them to preach to his Mercian subjects, if any wished to hear them. He had so far softened his attitude towards Christianity, that all he now demanded was that if any of his subjects became Christians, they must be Christians indeed. "He hated and despised those who professed and called themselves Christians, and did not shew forth the works of faith. They were despicable wretches who did not obey the God in whom they believed." I always have a kindly feeling for this downright old pagan.

Two years after this, in the year 655, Penda's oppression of Oswy passed the bounds

of endurance. They were connected by the
double tie of inter-marriage; the son of each
was husband of a daughter of the other. But
nothing of that kind was allowed to stand
in Penda's way. Family relationships had
no avail to prevent or mitigate the warlike
operations of the Angles or the Saxons; and
it is evidently very doubtful whether in this
nineteenth century, or in the early twentieth,
such ties will have more avail. Penda de-
vastated Oswy's province almost to the point
of complete destruction. Four years before,
he had got so far as to besiege the royal
fortress of Bamborough, and had put in exe-
cution a method for its destruction which
those of us who know the position of that
noble rock-city can appreciate. Being unable
to get at the wooden stockade which crowned
the precipitous rock, he got together from all
the villages round an enormous collection of
inflammable material, beams, planks, wattle,
thatch, and whatever else would burn; piled
them up on the land side; and when the
wind blew from the land on to the stockade,
he set fire to the mass. Following upon Aidan's prayers, when from his place on Lindisfarne he saw what was happening, the
wind suddenly changed, and blew the fire and

smoke upon the besiegers, who fled in confusion.

Now, in 655, the audacity and violence of Penda was greater than ever. Oswy offered him incredibly large bribes if only he would go home and leave Northumbria in peace. Penda would not desist, for he had determined to obliterate Oswy's nation, leaving neither young nor old surviving. "If the pagan will not accept our gifts, we will offer them to One who will." So spake Oswy; and he vowed to dedicate to perpetual virginity his little daughter Elfleda, scarce a year old, a second Elfleda, and to give twelve estates for establishing twelve monasteries. Penda, as we have seen, was slain. Elfleda was dedicated to God, and after a noviciate at the Monastery of Heruteu, the Hart's Isle, now Hart-le-pool, she died Abbess of Whitby at the age of 60, in the year 714, when Bede was a man of nearly fifty. The twelve monasteries were duly founded, six in Deira and six in Bernicia.

King Oswy took possession of Mercia, and ruled it in right of conquest. Diuma, the Scotic priest already named, was made Bishop of the Middle Angles, whom Peada governed, and also of the Mercians under Oswy, and of the people of Lindsey, the "Lindisfaras," a word so like "Lindisfarners" in the Latin that some grievous mistakes have resulted from the likeness. He was consecrated by Finan. Bede explains—these little explanations of his, of ecclesiastical anomalies, are of very great value as shewing the feeling of the age as to what was natural—that the paucity of priests was the cause of one prelate being set over two nations, the Middle Angles and the Mercians.

This was the beginning of the great Midland see of Lichfield, the mother of twelve or of thirteen sees. Diuma only ruled the see for two years, when he died, and was buried among the Midland Angles at Feppingum, which has been doubtfully identified with Repton, Repton being then the capital of Mercia proper.

It will be seen that not even in the most indirect way can any connection be traced with the Italian mission in all these affairs, or any sort of reference to Canterbury or to Rome. The Italian influence, and the influence of Kent, were entirely absent from the whole of the vast domains of which we have to-day been speaking, Northumbria and Mercia. The same was true, as we have seen, of the whole of Wessex, the next largest portion of England; and also of Essex. In this year 655, sixty years after the first despatch of the Italian mission, Northumbria, Mercia, the East Saxon kingdom, and Wessex, were all ruled by prelates of Irish or of Scotic consecration; the teaching of Christianity was entirely in the hands of men of the pre-Augustine Churches of these islands, the Celtic Church and the Scotic Church. And in Mercia this went on. Ceollach, of Scotic race and consecration, succeeded Diuma at Lichfield in 658. The next year, 659, Ceollach returned to Iona, and Trumhere succeeded him. Trumhere, as his name indicates, was an Englishman; but Bede specially tells us that he was consecrated bishop in the Scotic Church. The Italians at Canterbury and Rochester were left severely—perhaps contemptuously—alone. They had been unsuccessful as missionaries in larger fields, when tried. And they were doubtless hampered by the fact that the supremacy under whose auspices they began their career had long passed away from Kent, and they and theirs were politically unimportant.

King Oswy made over to his son-in-law Peada the government of the South Mercians, that is, the Mercians south of Trent, in addition to his original kingdom of the Middle Angles. But in the next spring Peada was assassinated in a very nefarious manner, during the Easter festival; by the treachery, it was said, of his own Anglian wife. Oswy, it would appear, ruled, after that, the whole of the great midland kingdom, sending princes of the nature of viceroys. Three years after Peada's death, the three chief men of the Mercians rose against the foreign rule, expelled Oswy's viceroys, and set up Wulfhere, a son of Penda, now reaching man's estate. whom they had up to that time kept concealed. Wulfhere played a large part in the religious and political affairs of England. He was the greatest man of his time. His name is on the Bewcastle Cross, on account of his near relationship by marriage with Alchfrith.

When Wulfhere began to reign, he found himself without a bishop, by the retirement of Ceollach; what had made him retire, we are not told. He got his new bishop from Northumbria, Trumhere, Abbat of Gilling near Richmond, not the Gilling near Malton; and he had him consecrated in the Scotic Church. Trumhere was only bishop three years, and in 662 he was succeeded by Jaruman, whose origin we do not know, but he was clearly of the Scotic school. In this same year, 662, Wulfhere, as over-lord of the East Saxons, sold to Wini, Bishop of Wessex under the changeable Coinwalch, the bishopric of London; the first transaction of the kind of which we hear in our history. Three years later Wulfhere played a very different part for us Londoners, sending his bishop Jaruman to effect the final turning of the East Saxons from the worship of idols. And in 681 he persuaded Ethelwalch, the pagan king of the pagan South Saxons, to be baptized, and stood godfather to him, receiving him as he emerged from the font. As overlord of Wessex, he gave to Ethelwalch, in token of his adoption as his spiritual son, two important provinces, the Isle of Wight, and the land of the Meanwaras in Hampshire. Clearly he was a man of great power, and active in Christian work. His hand was felt all over, and it carried Christian influence with it.

When Jaruman died, in 667, things had greatly changed in England. The Council of Whitby had been held. The work of the Scotic Church in England was done. It had been noble work, that best of all work which is done exactly when it is wanted, just when no one else can or will do it. It was done. The Scotic bishop had withdrawn from Lindisfarne, and Chad had conformed to the Catholic use. There were in the whole of English England only three bishops,—the simoniacal Wini of the East Saxons, who died in 675; Boniface of the East Anglians, who died in 669; and Wilfrith, who had been consecrated bishop by Agilbert and eleven bishops at Compiegne, and was now exercising a sort of roving commission in Kent during the five years' vacancy at Canterbury. For two years Wulfhere did without a bishop of his own, the useful Wilfrith doing what he could for him. When Theodore came, in the end of May 669, there was no one else to apply to for a bishop, and Wulfhere set the example of recognising Canterbury as the natural ecclesiastical centre and head of the English Church [1]. He had been a warm supporter of the Scotic Church and its bishops; he now applied to Canterbury for help, and asked Theodore to send him a bishop. If Wulfhere had really no one else to apply to, Theodore had really no one to send. Roches-

---

[1] For the very different view of one of his successors, Offa, see p. 127.

ter had been vacant as long as Canterbury itself, nearly five years, and he had to fill that vacancy. He found Putta, an unworldly recluse and musician, and consecrated him. Dunwich fell vacant, too, in his first year here, and Bisi was found and consecrated to that see. For the Mercian see he had no one ready. So short of men was he, that from 669 to 672, although there were only two bishops in all England besides the two whom he consecrated in his first year, he only consecrated one bishop, and that a Frenchman sent over from Paris. To Wulfhere's request for a bishop he replied by asking Oswy to allow Chad to go from Northumbria to Mercia, and Chad's vacancy in Northumbria made room for Wilfrith there. So he tided over the dearth of men, and in the years 672 to 685 inclusive he consecrated seventeen bishops to thirteen sees. It is proposed that the work of Theodore, and the work of Wilfrith, shall form the subjects of a course of lectures next winter. For the present we can leave the conversion of Mercia an accomplished fact.

Theodore's treatment of Chad was creditable to both of them. When Theodore made his progress to the north, on his arrival in England, a step which indicates that he knew where the centre of gravity of importance was, he met with Ceadda[1], and upbraided him with the irregularity of his consecration. Ceadda, with great humility replied, "If thou knowest that I have not rightly received the office of bishop, I gladly withdraw from the office. I never thought myself worthy of it, and only as a matter of obedience did I undertake it." Theodore was moved by such gentle humility; declared that Chad must not lay down the episcopal office; and himself consummated anew his consecration in the Catholic manner.

It seems fairly clear from the phrase used that the original consecration was not radically bad; there was, in Theodore's opinion, some ritual flaw, when the consecration was tested by his Roman statute, something left undone which that statute required, or something not rightly done; and this defect Theodore supplied. The presumption is that it was something added by the Roman Church, not of catholic and fundamental necessity. We know how Rome has made such additions to the Ordinal, and how the Romans now assert that they are fundamental. The

---

[1] That is, Chad.

phrase used by Wilfrith's chaplain, Eddi, is very much stronger; he says that Chad was re-ordained through all the ecclesiastical degrees. We rather expect polemical statements from that quarter, and Bede is a better informant. Besides, if Theodore re-ordained Chad deacon and priest, he would have to re-ordain a great many priests and deacons; and we have no suggestion of that.

It is a fortunate thing that we know from Bede, incidentally so far as its connection with this episode is concerned, exactly how Chad was originally consecrated. What the flaw was, it is not easy to say. Oswy appointed Ceadda to be Bishop of the Church of York, the first after Paulinus. This was in 664. Ceadda went south to be consecrated, but he found that Deusdedit of Canterbury was dead, and no one was as yet put in his place. He went then to the province of the West Saxons, and was consecrated by Wini, who was of French consecration; the only bishop then in all Britain who was canonically consecrated, Bede says. What Bede can mean by this, it is not at all easy to say. We are dealing with a very late period of the year 664, for there had been time for Wilfrith to be chosen bishop after the Conference of Whitby in 664, and go abroad for consecration, and leave the way open for Chad to be put in his place; time, too, for Tuda to be consecrated by the South Irish bishops, after the Conference of Whitby, and to die, and for Chad to fill his place too. We may therefore suppose that Bishop Cedd of the East Saxons, Chad's brother, was dead, though he died as late as October 26. Damian, too, of Rochester, died in 664, no doubt at an earlier part of the year. But how can Boniface of Dunwich, who was consecrated in 652 and died in 669, have been rejected or forgotten by Bede? Ithamar seems to have passed him over when he consecrated Deusdedit in 655, but there can have been no doubt of the validity of his consecration. Bede's phrase "in all Britain" must be taken to be exhaustive; otherwise we might perhaps have pressed the name "Saxony," by which he calls East Anglia, as an explanation. The modern East Anglian would reject the explanation that Dunwich was hopelessly out of the world, and its bishop was out of sight and out of mind. However that may have been, Wini, too, passed him over. He desired to have the canonical number of three consecrating bishops, and he called two British bishops to be partakers in the consecration, un-orthodox in their Easter.

These were the facts. What was the flaw which Theodore discovered? Some suggestions can be made. If Wini consecrated Ceadda in his capacity of Bishop of the West Saxons, we must look beyond Wini for the flaw. But if he had had time to buy the bishopric of the East Saxons, he was in a technical sense a simoniacal bishop, and it is conceivable that even so early as that ordinations by a simoniacal bishop were regarded by some as invalid. It is significant that when Theodore held the Council of Hertford in 673, he recited in a preamble to the proceedings the names of the bishops present or represented by proxies, and no mention is made of Wini or of the East Saxons, though part of Hertford was actually in that kingdom. This may mean that Theodore would not recognise Wini as bishop, but did not feel able to depose him, as he did depose Winfrid of Mercia soon after for disobedience. On the other hand, political considerations may have accounted for the absence of the East Saxon bishop and king.

There remains the fact, carefully mentioned

by Bede, that Wini, not acting alone, but not having any canonically consecrated bishops within reach, took to him, as associates in the consecration[1], two bishops of the nation of the Britons, who kept Easter from the 14th to the 20th of the moon, according to their custom. We gather from Aldhelm that they were of the Cornish and Devon line of British bishops. In these days, when, in order to have a second string to their bow in the attack upon Archbishop Parker's consecration, our Roman friends declare that the soundness of the episcopal orders of co-consecrators can not validate a consecration where there is a flaw in the orders of the chief consecrator, for that only the chief consecrator consecrates, it seems a little too much to argue that a flaw on the part of the co-consecrators invalidates a consecration when the chief consecrator's orders are sound. Or again, in these days an objection might be taken that a consecration of a bishop ought not to take place when there is a vacancy in the metropolitical see; but any such objection is an anachronism when applied to Wini's time. Canterbury made no

---

[1] "In societatem ordinationis," Bede iii. 28.

such claim as that in those days. I am inclined to think it was Wini's ritual rather than his or his colleagues' ecclesiastical position that was in question. If it was the British bishops that invalidated the consecration, then I think we can quote Theodore against the modern Romans in their attack upon Parker.

The descent of the numerous Mercian sees from Lichfield is rather complicated.

In 656 the see of Lichfield was established, as we have seen, during Oswy's rule, in the person of Diuma. For twenty years there was only one bishop's see in Mercia. Then, on Theodore's principle of subdivision, a very great change took place. The Northumbrian king Ecgfrith had for a time won back from Mercia the long-disputed province of Lindsey, roughly speaking, Lincoln, and it was made a separate Northumbrian see under Eadhed in 678; but it counted in early history practically as a Mercian see. The see of Lindsey disappeared by union with Dorchester about the year 1000.

The see of Hereford, marking an extension of Mercia to the south and west, was formed two years before that of Lindsey, in 676. It came about in a curious way. Ethelred,

King of the Mercians, ravaged Kent, and destroyed the church of Rochester. Putta, the bishop, was absent; and, hearing that his church and his personal property were all gone, he did not return to Rochester. We have seen that he was not at all a man of the world; a musical recluse, not a man with fight in him. Saxulf, the Mercian bishop, settled him in Mercia, no doubt in a very small way, in a new see, which we call Hereford. There he lived and taught church-music, being extraordinarily skilled in the Roman style, which he had learned from scholars of Pope Gregory. Of Hereford we need say no more.

Four years after this, in 680, the province of the Wiccii was made a bishop's see. We call it Worcester. Here again no more need be said.

In the same year, Lichfield itself was subdivided, and a Bishop of Leicester was appointed, Cuthwin. He was bishop from 680 to 691, and then the Northumbrian Wilfrith administered the see from 691 to 705. It was then united with Lichfield from 705 to 737, and in 737 was again made an independent see. About 888 Dorchester (near Oxford), of which we spoke under Wessex, was added, and so the enlarged see went on to the Conquest, when Remigius was made the first Norman bishop, called of Dorchester. He moved his bishop's seat to the hill of Lincoln, in Lindsey, where it still remains. To pursue the history of this part of the Mercian territory, in 1109 Ely was formed, with part of East Anglia and part of Mercia; and at the Reformation the enormous diocese of Lincoln was reduced in size by the establishment of Peterborough (parts of which had in earlier times counted as East Anglia) in 1541, and Oseney in 1542. Oseney became the see of Oxford in 1545.

Turning now to Lichfield proper, from which Leicester was taken in 737, a see of Chester was formed in 1075, and Coventry in 1102. The name of the see has varied considerably, the name of Lichfield being at times dropped. In 1541, the present independent see of Chester was formed, and assigned to the province of York.

Southwell has, in very recent times, relieved Lichfield of Derbyshire, and the modern Lincoln of Nottinghamshire, formerly in the province of York to which the great church of Southwell belonged. Southwell is a hybrid see, the early ecclesiastical records of the

Derbyshire portion being at Lichfield in the province of Canterbury, and those of the Nottinghamshire portion at York itself.

Wulfhere and Diuma will appear in our transept windows. Chad appears under Northumbria.

In speaking of the ecclesiastical arrangements of Mercia, it is impossible altogether to omit mention of the curious fact that it was once made an archiepiscopal province. The royal family of Kent became extinct in the battle of Otford, and Offa the Mercian king assumed royal authority in that kingdom. The Archbishop of Canterbury was the greatest person in the kingdom of Kent, and indeed, next to kings, in all the land of England; and Offa desired that his own Bishop of Lichfield should be at least as great. It was no doubt anomalous that a small and subject state should rule ecclesiastically over his great and victorious kingdom. He obtained the consent of his bishops and Witenagemot, and declared Higbert archbishop. To give him rank with Canterbury and York, he applied for the pall to the Pope. "The apostolic see," Matthew of Paris remarks in relating the circumstances, " never fails a man who gives plenty of money;" and in this case he says the money given was "infinite." The thing was done about the year 787. The opportunity was taken by the Pope to send papal legates, who adopted the airs of supremacy. Canterbury was deprived of all its property and its suffragans in Mercian territory. We have no contemporary account of the sees actually taken away, but the statement of William of Malmesbury seems reasonable, that the only suffragans left to Canterbury were London, Rochester, Winchester, Sherborne, and Selsey. Those were the bishops of Kent, the East and Middle Saxons, the West Saxons, and the South Saxons. The Northern Province and the Midland Province would thus be all Angles; the Southern Province all Saxons and Jutes. It was on rather scandalous proceedings that the exercise of papal supremacy in England was by degrees built up. The Mercian archbishopric only lasted about sixteen years. All was set straight again in 803, under Leo III, who did not scruple to undo, as wrongly done and sanctioned, the greatest ecclesiastical change a Pope ever made or sanctioned in England.

The Council of the English Church held at Clofesho (October 12, 803) made no scruple of using very strong language about the impropriety of the original transaction. It is true that they laid the blame directly on Offa, and did not name the Pope; but equally they claimed that it was done by the king's self-will, and did not suggest that any one else had any real power in the matter. Offa had "presumed most fraudulently to divide and cleave the honour and the unity of the see of our father the holy Augustine in the city of Canterbury." When Ethelheard succeeded Jaenberht, the act of the Council proceeded to say, he went to the threshold of the apostles (*apostolorum*, not *apostoli*), and visited the most blessed Pope of the apostolic see, Leo. Among other important matters, he set out at length the unjust division of the archiepiscopal see. When the apostolic Pope heard and understood that it had been unjustly done, he at once called into play the full weight of his authority, and sent to Britain to say that the arrangement made by the holy Gregory must be restored. The Council of Clofesho rejected the charter of Pope Hadrian, as having been surreptitiously and by evil blandishments obtained.

The signatures of the archbishop and bishops

to the fourth[1] of the acts of this Council of Clofesho at which the old arrangement was restored, are interesting as shewing the different styles of description of bishoprics. The two East Anglian bishoprics afford one of the best illustrations of this difference, when considered in relation to the facts mentioned in Lecture III. A facsimile is given in *Anglo-Saxon MSS.* Part I, No. IV. (Master of the Rolls), 1878; and the whole is printed by Haddan and Stubbs, Vol. III., pp. 545-7. Ethelheard signs (i.e. attaches the sign of the cross to the statement written by the scribe, *Ego Æthelheardus gratia Dei Archiepiscopus Dorobernensis civitatis signum sanctae crucis subscripsi*) as Archbishop of the city of Dorobernum (Canterbury). The other descriptions are: Bishop of the Church of Lichfield; of the city of Leicester; of the city of Sidnacester (place unknown, meaning the See of Lindsey); of the city of Worcester; of the Church of Hereford; of the Church of Sherborn; of the city of Winton (Winchester); of the Church of Elmham; of the city of Dummuc (Dunwich); of the city of London;

---

[1] "Forbidding the election of laymen or seculars as lords of monasteries, against this our mandate and that of the lord apostolic Pope."

of the city of Rochester; of the Church of Selsey.

This act was passed "at the well-known place called Clofeshoas." It is not really known where this well-known place was.

LECTURE V.

THE EAST SAXONS

The bishopric.—Relapse into paganism.—Sigebert the Good and Oswy.—Scotic teachers of the faith sent to the East Saxons.—Cedd; his consecration.—Ythancester.—Sigebert's death.—Lastingau and Ethelwald.—Death of Cedd.—Second (partial) relapse into paganism.—Descent of the see of London.

It is natural that we in London should look with special interest to the details of the establishment of Christianity among our East Saxon ancestors. As a matter of fact, we were the most perverse and obstinate pagans of all the seven kingdoms.

The kingdom of the East Saxons was founded by Erchenwin about the year 527. Our bishopric is called, in the Anglo-Saxon lists to which reference has been made[1], the bishopric "of the East Saxons," not "of London." The principal text of the Anglo-Saxon Chronicle, under the year 604, says:

---

[1] See p. 64.

"This year the East Saxons received the faith and baptism under Sæbright king and Mellitus bishop." The longer form of the Chronicle says "Æthelberht gave Mellitus a bishop-settle at Lunden-town (Lunden-wic)." The distinction thus drawn was probably in the origin sound. It was the bishopric of the East Saxons, and its seat was London. There had been British bishops of London for a long time, as we have seen on other occasions[1], and the last of them had fled to the west only a few years before the coming of Mellitus, so far as we can gather from evidence not completely trustworthy; but so far as the English race and the Church of England are concerned, the English bishopric of London was founded in the person of Mellitus in 604.

Mellitus's church was St. Paul's, the forerunner of this St. Paul's. In 609, tradition tells us, Ethelbert, the over-lord of the East Saxons and uncle of the East Saxon king, gave for the maintenance of the fabric of the church the estate of Tillingham, in Essex, which we still hold for that same purpose; the only part of our vast property still held by us personally. In 616, as we saw last

---

[1] See *The Church in these Islands before Augustine*, S.P.C.K., p. 99.

year [1], the sons of our first Christian king of the East Saxons, Sabert, Ethelbert's sister's son, drove out Mellitus because he would not give them the sacramental bread, pagans as they were and not baptized. Twelve years of Italian episcopal work had not touched the younger generation of the royal family. The Italian bishop himself, Mellitus, fled to Gaul, and Christianity was blotted out. He returned, it is true, in the course of a year, but at the express command of the King of Kent. London refused to receive him, preferring the idolatrous priests. He lived at Canterbury for the rest of his life; became archbishop in 619; and died third archbishop of the English in 624.

From 616 to 653, no less than thirty-seven years, London and the kingdom of Essex remained pagan. Augustine and his companions, even the long-lived Honorius, all passed away, and yet we Londoners maintained our paganism. It was not till a Saxon archbishop, consecrated by a Saxon bishop, sat on Augustine's throne, that London was brought once more to the Christian obedience. The circumstances of its return were in them-

---

[1] See *Augustine and his Companions*, S.P.C.K., p. 163.

selves exceedingly interesting. That Bede's story is completely authentic we may take as certain. Bede was born before the king who brought about the restoration died; and his friend Nothelm, who sent him the account from the original records, was archpresbyter of London.

The pagan sons of Sabert were killed in battle. King Sigebert the Little reigned for some considerable time, and was succeeded by Sigebert surnamed the Good. Sigebert the Good was a friend of Oswy, King of Northumbria, Oswald's brother and successor; the king who presided, eleven years after the events of which we are about to speak, at the Synod of Whitby, dying eventually in 670 when his subject Bede was a little boy.

Sigebert the Good used frequently to visit Oswy, and Oswy used to argue with him about his religion. Bede tells us one of the main lines of his argument. "Those could not be gods that were made by the hands of men. A log or a stone could not be material for creating a god, the remnants of which were burned as firewood, or made into vessels for common use, or thrown out contemptuously and trodden into the ground. God must rather be regarded as incomprehensible in majesty, invisible to the eye of man, omnipotent, eternal; Who created the heaven and the earth and the race of man; Who ruled and would judge the world in equity. His eternal seat was not in vile and decaying matter, but in the heavens. It was rightly to be held that all who learned and did His will would receive from Him eternal rewards."

Many arguments of this kind Oswy as a friend and a brother urged upon Sigebert. At length his guest believed. He took counsel with his personal attendants, exhorted them that they likewise should believe, and obtained their assent. They were all baptized together by the Scotic bishop Finan of Lindisfarne, at a Northumbrian royal residence near the Roman wall, twelve miles from the sea. That puts it at or near Walbottle. My own predilection is for Benwell, on account of its name. The eastern extremity of the other wall, where it abuts upon the Firth of Forth not far from Abercorn, is Kinnell. Bede explains that in the Pictish tongue it was called Penfahel, in British Penguaul, compounds of the British Pen, *a head*, with a form of *vallum*, a wall. Kinnell is the Celtic equivalent, the Celts using a *k* or hard *c* where the Britons used a *p* or *b*, Ceanmore and Kenmore being the same word as Benmore, the great head[1]. Benwell is the British form of Kinnell, and means "the head of the wall," suitably called in Latin *ad murum*, "where the wall begins." The amusing controversy carried on with so much warmth in the sixth chapter of the *Antiquary* turns upon the derivation of the name of this place, which is there given as Benval.

From this it is quite clear that the conversion of Sigebert was due to the teaching and work of the Scotic Church, and had nothing whatever to do with the Italian mission, which had in fact died out, or with their Saxon successor at Canterbury. Mercia, as we saw two days ago, was converted by precisely this same influence, and its king was baptized at the very same place, and by the same Scotic bishop, Finan. Oswald, as we saw a week ago, was the sponsor of the King of Wessex, receiving him as he emerged from the font. Those two Scotic brothers, then, Oswald and Oswy, with their Scotic bishops Aidan and Finan, were the converting or re-converting influence in Northumbria, Mercia, the East

---

[1] See *The Church in these Islands before Augustine* S.P.C.K., p. 38.

Saxon kingdom, and Wessex:—almost the whole of England except four counties.

Sigebert returned to his royal residence among the East Saxons, the position of which we are not told. It may perhaps be safe to suppose that it was London, but London is not mentioned in the story, while two other places are. No doubt the kings then, as in later times, had several residences, and moved from one to another as the local supplies of food, collected at the royal vill or manse, were exhausted. The king begged Oswy to send him Christian teachers. Cedd was recalled to Northumbria from the work in Mercia, and was sent with another priest, whose name unfortunately is not recorded by Bede, to preach and baptize among the East Saxons. It is a fact eminently deserving attention that the king sent to the Tyne for a priest, and from the Tyne they sent to Lichfield for the man, when all the time there was a bishop (Ithamar) at Rochester, and he an Englishman, and a bishop (Boniface) at Dunwich. Honorius of Canterbury was probably dead, and the remarkable interregnum which followed his death had commenced and probably had not come to an end; but there were certainly priests left at Canterbury, and monks in considerable numbers. In these days of rapid communication, it does not seem to us so strange as it actually was in those days of laborious travel. But even with us, it is easier to ask a man to come from Canterbury, 62 miles, or Rochester, 32 miles, to preach at St. Paul's, than to fetch him from Newcastle, 272 miles, especially if he has first to travel from Lichfield to Newcastle, making 160 miles more. The facts shew, as it seems to me, an active consciousness of real opposition to foreign influences, to an extent which many persons do not recognise. And they throw very grave difficulties, from the historian's point of view, in the way of those who are now claiming that the Celtic Churches in Ireland and Scotland were founded by the direct action of Rome. With oral traditions of an accuracy at least as great as that of printed books, it is not really conceivable that all record of a deep debt due to Rome should have passed clean away; that practices not those of Rome should have been universal in the Celtic Churches; and the sole attitude of those Churches to Rome should be one of jealousy and suspicion and dislike. For Rome had not meanwhile been operating for centuries against their independence, and interfering in their affairs, and impoverishing their people, as she had done with England when we at the Reformation at last treated our great debt of gratitude as for the time at least more than cancelled. And there is a curiously decided absence of claim on the part of Rome in those days to have founded either the British or the Irish Church, or to have any right to that gratitude to which help in the time of infancy would have entitled her. I do not like to suggest that the conspicuous failure of the Canterbury Italians to effect a real lodgement in London had anything to do with Sigebert's action. There may no doubt have been political reasons for going to the north and not going to Canterbury, reasons connected with the relations existing among the three kingdoms of Essex, Kent, and Northumbria; but we do not know of really sufficient grounds on this side. Friendship with Oswy is scarcely a sufficient explanation for all the trouble taken, when the other course seems so easy in itself. The views thus suggested are decidedly confirmed by the fact that immediately after the Northumbrian Church had agreed to adopt the Catholic practices, Oswy of Northumbria and Ecgbert of Kent consulted together about the succession to Canterbury, and agreed upon the man. After that it is difficult to argue that political hostilities were the real cause.

The Anglian priest Cedd, sent thus by the Scotic Bishop Finan and the Scotic King Oswy to preach to the Saxons in these parts of ours, had great success. He and his brother priest perambulated all the country; they congregated much church, great church, to the Lord, Bede tells us. It fell out that on one occasion Cedd went away northwards, to revisit his home, and got as far as the church of Lindisfarne, by which probably is meant the Christian colony in that island, and had discourse with Bishop Finan. When Finan heard how greatly the work of the Gospel had been prospered to him, he made him bishop of the East Saxons, having summoned to his aid for the ministry of consecration two other bishops.

Thus the bishopric of the East Saxons was re-established by the Scotic Church; not by Canterbury, nor by Rome, directly or indirectly. The East Saxon see established by Augustine had been rooted up and done away. It was fifty years since Mellitus had been sent to London, thirty-eight years since he had been driven away, thirty-seven years since he had returned from France and been told that he was not wanted, "they preferred the idolatrous pontiffs." The Augustinian succession had been entirely unfruitful. We recite the name of Mellitus as first of the English succession of bishops of London. But the bishops of London do not count the succession of their orders from him or his; any more than the archbishops of Canterbury count the succession of their orders from Augustine or any of his companions.

Another point is worthy of mention. We see remarks, in partisan histories, on the irregular character of the Scotic Church, and its uncatholic habits, especially as regards the status and action of bishops. But here we have, from the Rome-loving hand of Bede, a full declaration of carefulness on a point of extreme importance. It is a point on which Augustine had shewn a disregard of catholic usage and law which would horrify Roman and Anglican alike if any bishop of the present day were to copy it. Augustine, with the full consent and authority of Gregory, that man of such strangely independent mind when a way out of a difficulty was to be found, Augustine had consecrated bishops alone. He had even, without consulting Gregory, consecrated his own successor to his own archiepiscopal see. Finan obeyed the Catholic rule that three bishops at the least must be combined in the consecration of a bishop.

In another respect Finan's action was not in accordance with catholic use, and in this respect the British and the Scotic Churches alike were from the nature of the case out of harmony with catholic practice. There was no metropolitan. Those churches had not, as most of us believe, a metropolitical organisation. There may have been a Primus, as in the Scottish Church of to-day, the bishops forming an Episcopal College; but if that was so, we get, I think, no hint of it in Bede. Finan, so far as we know, acted entirely on his own responsibility; and what business it was of his to consecrate in Northumbrian Lindisfarne a bishop for the East Saxon kingdom, I must leave others to say. If we did but know what his commission from Iona was, this and other puzzling questions might puzzle us no more. It is, of course, no explanation that the see of Canterbury was vacant, and there were not any signs of its being filled up, for the Northumbrian Church acted for many years in complete independence of the Church of Kent. Some writers give 658 as the date of Cedd's consecration[1]. If that is correct, then there was an archbishop at Canterbury, a Wessex man, not an Italian.

The law of the Church of England, as formulated by Henry VIII, is strictly catholic in respect of provincial consecrations. If there was a vacancy in both archbishoprics, and at the same time a bishopric was vacant, one of the archbishoprics must be filled before the consecration of a bishop to the vacant bishopric could take place. The most anarchical time the Church in England has ever known in this respect, since Augustine and Gregory, was the time of Queen Mary and Cardinal Pole, when for years there was no archbishop of Canterbury, as Rome would say, and at least no commission from an archbishop, and bishops were uncanonically intruded into sees. At Queen Elizabeth's accession, several of the Roman bishops of English dioceses were not canonically bishops of the dioceses into which they had been intruded. The list usually given of expulsions of bishops by Elizabeth has to be considerably discounted

---

[1] Lumby and Mayor, *Bede*, iii. and iv., p. 424.

from this point of view. It is in fact only just as long as the list of Queen Mary's expulsions.

As to who the bishops were whom Finan called to himself for the ministry of consecration, we must presume that they were Scotic bishops. The British bishops were out of the question. The Britons and the Angles of the North were at daggers drawn in the most literal sense; a state of things probably—indeed certainly—quite different from that which existed in the relations of Wessex and Cornwall when two British bishops helped Wini to consecrate Cedd's brother, Chad. Bede does not suggest that Finan had any difficulty in finding two bishops to join him in the consecration of Cedd. One point more, of the many which the consecration of Cedd raises or settles. Bede has no conception of the modern Roman theory that only the principal bishop consecrates, and those who are joined with him are only there for the practical purpose of full witnesses. The two bishops were called by him to himself for the ministry of consecration [1].

Cedd returned to his work among our ancestors, and made full profit of the greater

[1] "Vocatis ad se in ministerium ordinationis aliis duobus episcopis." H. E. iii. 22.

authority he now possessed. He built churches in several places, and ordained priests and deacons to help him in preaching and baptizing. He formed two principal centres of work, neither of them in London. As Aidan and Finan settled not at inland York, from which place Paulinus had fled, but at a new place on the sea, Holy Isle, so Cedd did not choose London, but made his chief centres at Ythancestir, on the banks of the river Pente, and at Tilbury, called in his time Tilaburg, on the banks of the Thames. Ythancestir has been placed near Maldon, but it almost certainly was much nearer to the actual coast. It was an important station in the Roman times, one of the coast fortresses, Othona. To see how nearly allied the names are, we must remember that a *y* was practically a short *u*, and I suppose the second *o* in Othona was pronounced short. About thirty years ago they were reclaiming land from the sea near Bradwell, at the N.E. corner of the Dengie Hundred, and they came upon the foundations of a great Roman fortress, with walls fourteen feet thick [1], enclosing between three and four acres, and horse-shoe

---

[1] This is the thickness of the solid towers at Burghcastle, see p. 88.

towers. Vast quantities of Roman remains were found, and many coins of the third and fourth centuries. Here, we cannot doubt, was Ythancestir; and its nearness to Tillingham seems to shew that in the times of which we are speaking the centre of gravity of importance lay towards that part of the East Saxon land, and had by no means as yet settled itself at or near London. It is of course quite possible, perhaps probable, that the gift of Tillingham had not been withdrawn in the confusion of the relapse. It had certainly not been forgotten; and if it needed renewing, Sigebert would naturally renew it. Cedd's choice of a place of residence may well have been guided by that gift. The name of the river Pente, curiously enough, lingers still, one of the springs which form the source of the Freshwell being called Pant's Well; indeed the name of the Freshwell itself is said to have been Pant in former times.

The chief centre of Cedd's episcopal work was Ythancestir. It was here in particular that the priests and deacons whom he ordained were to help him in the word of faith and the ministry of baptizing. It is evident from the phrase employed by Bede that his clergy were not imported from the north; they were native East Saxons, trained by himself. At Tilbury—it seems strange to think of the banks of the Thames as the remote place and the banks of the Pente as the busy populous place—he formed a monastic establishment, gathering a flock of servants of Christ, and teaching them to observe the discipline of the regular life, so far as those rude people were as yet fit for it.

After some considerable time Sigebert the Good was murdered by two of his relatives. They assigned as the sole cause of their act that they were enraged with the king for the excess which he shewed in sparing his enemies, and the readiness with which he forgave those who had injured him and asked his pardon. It is delightful to hear that his life was so truly Christian. He deserves the name of Sigebert the Martyr, as well as that of Sigebert the Good. Bede characteristically points out that his death was in fact a punishment for a serious error. The story seems to shew the difficulties of missionaries in those days as in these, in a matter which still gives rise to much discussion in the missionary field. One of the assassins, "counts" Bede calls them, had contracted an unlawful marriage; and inasmuch as the bishop could not prevent it, and had not secular power to correct it, he excommunicated the count. The king made light of this, and went to feast with his count. Riding away from the feast he met the bishop, who also was on horseback. The king dismounted. So did the bishop. The king threw himself on the ground at the bishop's feet, and begged for pardon. But the bishop was full of wrath; and touching the king with the rod he held in his hand, he declared with pontifical authority,—" Forasmuch as thou wouldest not refrain thyself from the house of that man, lost and condemned, in that very house thou shalt die." Bede's concluding remark on this punishment of Sigebert's fault by death is a little difficult. "His death not only blotted out the offence, but also increased his merit, for it happened in consequence of his piety and his observance of the commands of Christ."

Sigebert's successor, Suidhelm, was baptized by Cedd at the court of the East Anglian king, a place called then and still called Rendelsham; Ethelwald, king of the East Angles, brother to Anna, stood sponsor. This is an interesting hint of a larger degree of inter-communion between two kingdoms and two dioceses than we should have expected.

The passage by sea and land from Bradwell to Rendelsham is only about forty miles.

Cedd continued to pay visits to his northern home. Ethelwald, who governed the Deiri, Oswald's son, begged him to accept a site and build a monastery in Deira, to which the king might frequently resort to pray to God and hear His word, and where he might be buried. He believed, too, that he would be much helped by the daily prayers of those who there should serve God. Cedd chose a place in the recesses of the hills, near Kirby Moorside in Yorkshire, called then Lastingau. There he built the monastery, with the help of his brother Celin, Ethelwald's favourite chaplain, and of Cynebil, yet another brother, making, with Chad, an interesting group of four brethren. He appointed provosts, and came himself to sojourn there when he could. Utta, as we have seen[1], took the princess Elfleda by sea from Kent to Northumbria, and we may with probability imagine that Cedd's journeys were made by the same way. The ship that carried Oswy's bride must itself have passed very near Bradwell, as a glance at the map shews, and that line of

[1] Page 107.

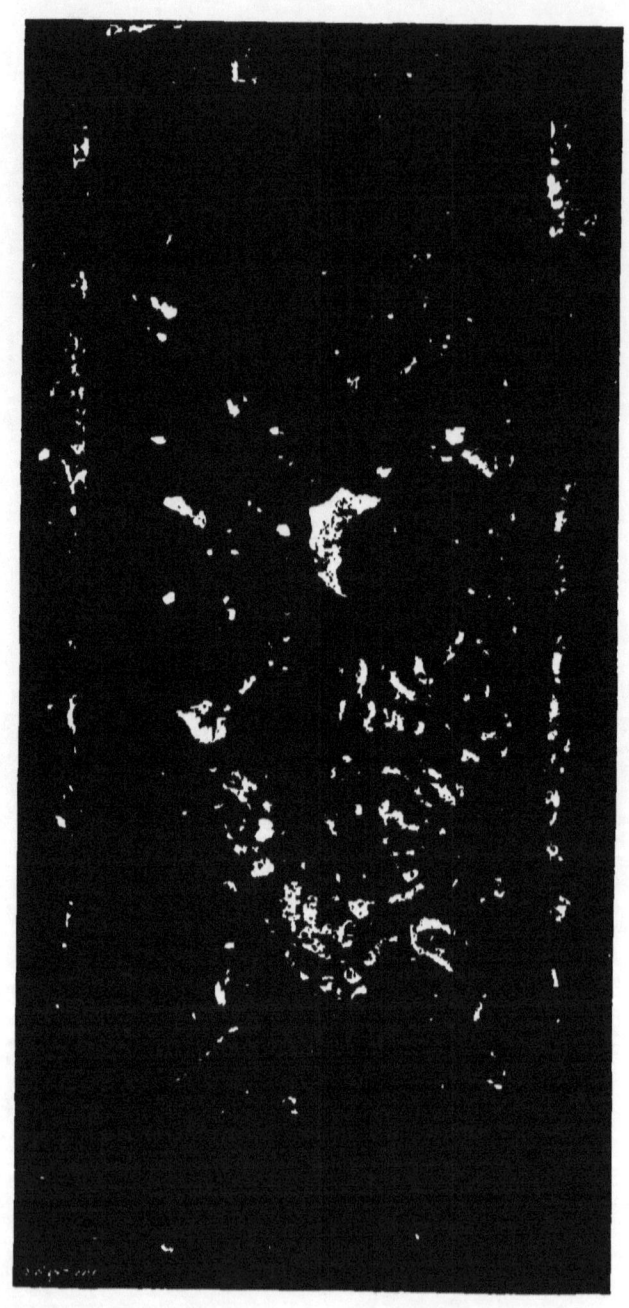

1. Cross-Slab of Oidilwald.

communication would suit Cedd very well. He may have gone round Spurn Point up the Humber, and landed as Tostig's northern allies did at Riccall, the ship stopping short of the Foul Ford; or he may even have pushed up the Derwent and so come by water very near to Lastingau; or, passing the Humber mouth, he would find Whitby a convenient landing-place, or one of the bays short of that. On one of his visits to Lastingau a plague broke out, and he died. They buried him at first in the open air, but when a stone church was built, dedicated to the Virgin Mary, he was buried at the right side of the altar.

It is too readily assumed that Lastingham is the exact place of Lastingau. In the repairs of Kirkdale Church, near Kirby Moorside and near Lastingham, a very beautiful slab was found, with a raised cross sculptured on it, and arabesques of foliage[1]. In the four angles of the cross were runes, legible at the time of its discovery, spelling *kununc Oithilwalde*, " to King Ethelwald." It has now perished, and when I had photographs taken of it ten years ago there was only one rune left, the "Oi" of the King's name. I have

---

[1] See figure 1, opposite.

seen, however, the drawing made of the letters when the stone was found, and many of them were still legible when the Rev. Daniel Haigh worked at the stone. This stone and the one next mentioned are very serious warnings against an error which has cost archæology dear. A stone a thousand or twelve hundred years old is dug out of earth of an antiseptic character, its ornament, and its inscription if it has one, clear and perfect; and it is assumed that a stone which has lasted so long will never decay. The stone is exposed to climatic conditions from which it has for many hundred of years been protected, and it rapidly decays. Another beautiful slab was found at the same time, of completely different type of ornament[1]. It was covered with bold and skilful interlacements, of the Lindisfarne type, and was without a name or inscription of any kind, so far as could be seen. These two stones are so remarkable, indeed, when taken together they are quite unique, that I ascribe the one to this King Ethelwald, and the other to our Bishop Cedd. I do not mean that they were sculptured at the time of their death: it was probably

---

[1] See figure 2, opposite.

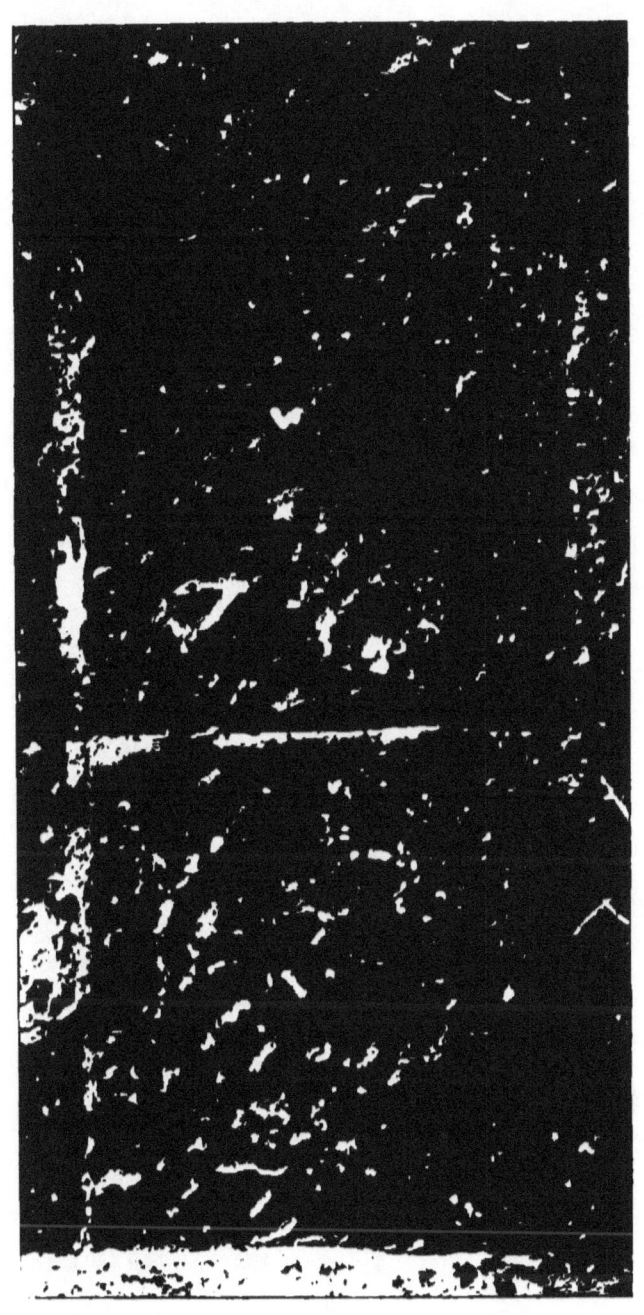

2.—Tombstone at Kirkdale Church.

not for twenty years after that event that work of this beautiful kind was developed by our Northumbrian ancestors. These slabs were probably sculptured when the stone church was built, and were used as the ornamental covers of the graves of the king and the bishop, north and south of the altar.

King Ethelwald's grave-cover was so very beautiful, that when I was asked about a design for Bishop Lightfoot's grave in Auckland Chapel I suggested this design, in which the bishop had been greatly interested when I shewed it to him. The suggestion was adopted, and was carried out in a very sympathetic manner. If my theory about Cedd's sepulchral stone is sound, it is pleasant to think of this close connection between the sculptured memorials of one of the very earliest of our Bishops of London and one of the most distinguished of our Canons of St. Paul's, an episcopal descendant of Finan who consecrated Cedd. I need not enter here upon a discussion of the date of this slab from the point of view of ornament. The shape of the cross itself is typical of the early shapes of crosses in Northumbria, and the foliage scroll has early counterparts. Of the other slab it is enough to say that designs of this beautiful and intricate description must have been very carefully studied in the Anglian School of Art at Lindisfarne through many of the later years of that century, before the Lindisfarne Gospels could be decorated as they are.

There are some difficulties about the date of Cedd's death. Bede remarks that he ceased to follow the Scottish ways, that is, he accepted the decision of the Council of Whitby, at which he was present and acted as interpreter, and thus we East Saxons were at once brought into line with the Catholic usages. And then, Bede adds, he returned to his see [1]. And yet he died at Lastingau (on Oct. 26) in this same year 664. It seems very unlikely that he should have made the journey between Essex and Yorkshire three times in less than half a year. He went north for the synod, which certainly took place some considerable time after Easter, for it was the special difficulty of the incidence of Easter in that year that led to the synod. The king was keeping the Scotic Easter Day while the queen was keeping the Catholic Palm Sunday. To summon all the important people, and

---

[1] "Ad sedem suam," iii. 26.

allow them time for the journey, must have brought the synod well on in the summer. Then, it seems, he returned to his see. Then he went north again, caught the plague, and died. I do not know how far it is safe to suggest that his *sedes* may in this case mean his monastery at Lastingham, to which, in that supposition, he retired after the conference. This difficulty would disappear if we accepted the date 668 for Cedd's death, but other difficulties would take its place.

The pestilence that was fatal to Cedd was for a time fatal to his work among the East Saxons. It spread to our parts. King Sighere and that part of the East Saxon land which he ruled, relapsed into idolatry. He and his people, high and low, loving this life and not desiring or not believing the life that is to come, renewed the deserted shrines and adored images; as though they might thus be preserved from the pestilence. But Sebbe, the joint-king, with those over whom he ruled, kept devotedly the faith which they had received. I venture to make the suggestion that here we have a hint which explains the silence of the records as to any work being done by Cedd in London. I suspect that not being able to cover all the ground he had treated London as hopeless in its carelessness about the Christian faith and the future life, and confined himself to the eastern parts; and that Sighere and his people represented the irreligion of London, passing easily into paganism, while Sebbe and his deserted subjects represented the faithful work of Cedd.

Wulfhere, the Mercian king, was now the over-lord of the East Saxons. He sent his Scotic bishop, Jaruman, who had presumably conformed, to recall to the true faith that part of the province which was corrupted. A priest who was Jaruman's companion on this occasion described to Bede, many years after, the energy and discretion with which the bishop Jaruman carried out his difficult commission. The result was that king and people joined in forsaking or destroying the shrines and altars they had made; opened the churches again; and joyfully confessing the name of Christ, would rather die in the belief of the resurrection in Him, than live among idols in the vileness of apostasy.

Thus was London finally brought to the true faith, in or about the end of the year 664, just sixty years after Mellitus was first sent here by Augustine. There is no other example in our history of pagan perversity so obstinate and so long as this of our own London.

Of Cedd's successor, Wini, I have already spoken[1]. We are not proud of this simoniacal bishop, and some of the Anglo-Saxon lists omit him altogether. As we have seen, he did not appear at Theodore's Council of Hertford; and it has been suggested that Theodore declined to recognise him on account of his simoniacal entry upon the see. It is, however, more probable that political reasons made the East Saxon king and bishop absent from the Council. He died in 675, and then our first sainted bishop came, Erkenwald. Erkenwald's shrine was the great treasure of St. Paul's till the time of the Reformation. The account of its splendour is mournful reading to the present nominal treasurer, who no longer has that magnificent *trésor* in his keeping. Till the time of the fire we had in St. Paul's the sarcophagus which held the good king Sebbe's bones.

Mellitus as the founder, and Cedd as the restorer, of East Saxon Christianity, will appear in our transept window of the twelve

---

[1] See pp. 59, 120, &c.

primary bishops of the English kingdoms. And Sabert and Sigebert will appear among the twelve primary kings. With these will be associated King Sebbe and St. Erkenwald.

The descent of the diocese of the East Saxons has been almost irritating in its contradictions. The Bishop of the East Saxons with his seat at London has ceased to have Essex in his diocese. It was given, not so very long ago, by one of the worst of many bad re-arrangements, to Rochester; and then, again in our own recollection, to a new bishopric, that of St. Albans. The Bishopric of London is now concentrated upon Middlesex. The time seems to be coming near for the original intention of Gregory to be carried out, by the establishment of an Archbishopric of London, with at least six diocesan suffragans. If the ecclesiastical authorities made London north and south of the Thames all one, the civil authorities would soon follow, and we should see a real unification.

LECTURE VI.

SUSSEX, AND CONCLUDING REMARKS.

The South Saxon land.—Bosham.—Wilfrith.—Ethelwalch and Ebba.—Wilfrith's success.—Selsey.—The South Saxon see.—The sons of Atwald.—The boy at Selsey.—Areas of England covered by the foreign and the Scotic missionaries respectively.—The British Church.—The celebration of the 1300th anniversary of the baptism of Ethelbert, in its true proportion.

WE have now come to the smallest and the latest of the English kingdoms; latest from the Christian point of view, but one of the earliest as a matter of secular history. It was the next in order of foundation to Kent, the earliest of all. It took high rank in the beginning, its founder, King Ælla, being counted by Bede as the first to exercise supremacy over the English in general. The date of this supremacy is given as 491. It is needless to say that at that early date the territories in actual possession by the English did not afford a very wide area for Ælla's supremacy.

The Anglo-Saxon Chronicle is brief and pithy on the subject of Ælla's proceedings. In 477, he and his three sons, Cymen, Wlencing, and Cissa, came to Britain in three ships, landed at Cymenes-ore, off-slew many Welsh (i.e. strangers, Britons), and drove some in flight into the wood called Andredeslea. In 485, Ælla fought against the Welsh (as before, Britons) near Mercredes-burnan-stede. In 490, Ælla and Cissa besieged Andredes-ceaster (Pevensey), and off-slew all that there dwelled, so that not one Bryt survived.

Bede puts the land of the South Saxons as a land of 7,000 families, and the Isle of Wight, which was usually connected with it, though occupied by Jutes not by Saxons, as a land of 1,200 families. Sussex, on the mainland, was thus equal in extent, or in ability to maintain a population, to the northern portion of Mercia, Mercia north of Trent, and the Isle of Wight was of a size or ability to maintain 120 monasteries. The dimensions of Sussex have not undergone change from that time. As kingdom, diocese, county, it has through all changes from that time to this preserved its identity; and in this it is unique in England.

We are, on the whole, in this course of lectures dealing with the period from 633 to 668. But if we were to confine ourselves to this period so far as the South Saxons are concerned, we should leave them alone in their inveterate paganism;—leave them alone, as, very strangely, Canterbury had done, and for long after 668 continued to do. There was no doubt a dense barrier of dangerous forest and marsh between Kent and the South Saxon land, and we know only too well the attitude of the Italian mission towards the idea of danger. Perhaps no further explanation need be sought. The South Saxons were shut off from the world by a belt of forest, represented as impassable, 120 miles long from east to west, and thirty miles deep. So far as ancient roads were concerned, we may fairly say that the best way to Sussex from anywhere was by sea. The great fortress of Anderida, now Pevensey, towards the east end, and the ancient city of Regnum, now Chichester, at the west end, had, we may suppose, some sort of pathway of communication northwards with the parts we call Surrey, through the immense forest of the Andredesleah; but it could at most be a communication that was very easily closed against unwelcome visitors, and road in any ordinary sense there was none. The marshes which covered the face of Kent on the extreme east of the narrow slip of South Saxon land, may have afforded at least some excuse for the curious inactivity of the Kentish Church through more than three-quarters of a century. Even so, the neglect seems inexplicable. And when the work was at last done, it was not done by or from Kent.

It was not till the year 681, when Kent had been Christian for eighty-four years, and even our obstinate London had been settled in the faith for about sixteen years, that an attempt was made to convert the South Saxons. How late in time and circumstance that was, may perhaps be gathered from the two facts, that the eightieth bishop of Rome then sat on the seat called of St. Peter, and that the sixth of the Great Councils of the Church was condemning the seventy-first bishop of Rome for heresy. It would appear that the South Saxons were not a very intolerable or desperate set of pagans; for when the attempt to christianise them was at last made, there was found to be a little Scotic monastery already there, under the charge of one Dicul, an Irishman, who had five or six monks with him. This was at Bosanham, now called Bosham[1], a place of extreme interest, with a Roman basilica for the foundation of its parish church, the details of which are shewn at the beginning of the Bayeux Tapestry, with the label *Ecclesia de Bosham*. It was at that spot that Harold took ship for the ill-fated voyage which ended in Brittany and led to Normandy. Of Dicul and his little party of monks we know nothing more than that they were Scotic; that they served the Lord in humility and poverty; and that none of the people of that province cared to imitate their life or to hear their preaching. Still, there they were; the Scotic Church yet once again, so late in time, modestly paving the way for men of another school.

In the year 681, then, a successful Christian teacher came at last. This was the famous

---

[1] The old pronunciation is clearly retained in the rustic *Baws-am*. It was this pronunciation that, according to the tale, obtained for the crafty Godwin this valuable manor. *Da mihi basium*, "Give me the kiss (of peace)," he is reported to have said to king Edmund. *Do tibi basium*, the king is said to have replied. On which Godwin thanked him, explaining that he had asked for Bosham, and Bosham the king had given.

Wilfrith, of Northumbria, whose history we are leaving to be treated if all be well next year. He had already gone through many of the fluctuations of his stormy career, and, finding himself an unwelcome visitor in most parts of the world, and specially unwelcome in the northern diocese which he regarded as his own, he was free to do anywhere the missionary work he did so well. Fuller likened him to the nightingale, which sings, Fuller said, ever the sweeter the further it is from home. Further from home, in England, Wilfrith could scarcely have been, than in Sussex; more sweetly and persuasively no one could have preached Christ to the South Saxons. Many years before, he had, in fact, been in Sussex. He was driven on shore there by a great storm, near high tide, on his way from Gaul to Kent; probably, therefore, at some point near the eastern extremity of Sussex. The barbarous people shewed them no little unkindness, claiming them and theirs as booty of the sea. Wilfrith's party defended themselves stoutly till the rising tide should float their ship, while Wilfrith and his clerks prayed. The pagan priest of the neighbourhood stood on a mound and practised enchantments to bind the wrecked men's hands. A lucky shot with a sling-stone slew the priest: the ship floated just in time, and they got off with a loss of five men. Probably Wilfrith did not introduce himself to the authorities, on the occasion of his second visit, as the man whose party slew their priest.

Ethelwalch, the king, was already a Christian. He had some time before paid a visit to Mercia, whose king appears to have had at that time considerable power in the South Saxon territory, as over-lord. The king was our old friend Wulfhere, who had done in his time such important services to the progress of Christianity; and as Wulfhere's reign came to an end in 672 or 673, Ethelwalch's visit to him must have been at least nine years before Wilfrith's arrival in Sussex. Wulfhere persuaded Ethelwalch to be baptized, and as his sponsor received him as he came up out of the font. In token of this spiritual adoption, Wulfhere gave to him two provinces, the Isle of Wight, namely, and the district of the Meonwaras[1] in Wessex. By what right Wulfhere owned or could give these territories, I do not think we really know. Ethelwalch returned to pagan Sussex

---

[1] See p. 62.

a Christian king, and as such for nine years at least he ruled a pagan land. His queen, Ebba, was a daughter of Eanfrid, prince of the Wiccas; roughly speaking, the people of Worcestershire. That province, as we have seen, was sufficiently advanced in Christianity to have a bishop of its own in 680, put there by the bishop of the main see of Mercia, and Ebba had been baptized in her own land before marrying Ethelwalch.

Here, then, Wilfrith found the way fully prepared. There was a Christian king, a Christian queen, and even a Christian monastery. I risk the suggestion that Wulfhere, who had good reason to know and be grateful for the missionary ability of the Scotic Church, had recommended Dicul[1] and his monks to Ethelwalch, as, twenty years before, Oswy had sent four Scotic teachers to Mercia, to begin the conversion of that great kingdom.

The king was delighted to give the new comer a free hand, and to see him baptize the chief governors and generals. The rest of the people were baptized, then and later

---

[1] Dicul was also the name of one of the two priests to whom Fursey left the charge of his monastery at Cnobheresburg.

on, by his four priests, Eappa, Padda, Burghelm, and Eadda.

Two things served to clench the hold which Wilfrith got upon the people of Sussex. There had been a terrible drought for three years, accompanied and followed by a famine so serious, that the starving people were driven to suicide. They would go by forty and fifty at a time to some precipice, or to the sea-shore, and hand-in-hand plunge over the precipice and be dashed to pieces, or walk into the sea and be drowned. But on the very day of the great baptizing just mentioned, there fell a quiet and copious rain; the earth blossomed forth again; a happy and abundant season followed. They cast off their old superstition; idolatry was completely driven away; their heart and their flesh rejoiced in the living God. They learned that He, who is the true God, by His heavenly grace endowed them with all good things, inward and outward. So Bede describes the effect which this coincidence produced.

The other thing which served to strengthen Wilfrith's hold upon them was of a different character. It was an example of Wilfrith's practical nature and varied and useful knowledge. Bede mentions it after the other, giving precedence to God's intervention; but it probably belongs to an earlier period in time. In the time of great famine, Wilfrith found that the people of the sea-coast did not understand the art of catching sea fish, which he, no doubt, had learned as a boy at Lindisfarne. They had eel-nets, but nothing more, though the sea and the rivers abounded in fish, which is still true as regards Sussex. The bishop's men borrowed a large number of eel-nets from the owners, fastened them together we must suppose, and cast them in the sea. They were so successful, that they quickly caught three hundred fishes, of one kind and another. These they divided into three equal parts, whether with any reference to that tripartite division of tithes which our disendowment friends so unsuccessfully seek to fasten upon the early English Church, it is for them rather than for me to say. They gave a hundred to the poor; a hundred to the owners of the eel-nets; and a hundred they kept for themselves. If you visit Bosham now, you will see how the marshy land is intersected by little winding creeks, and you will realise how small a net would suffice to close the mouth of one of the creeks, and, if the meshes were small enough, keep in the eels which had come in with the tide. The people, Bede tells us, when they found that by Wilfrith's temporal ministry they had gained such benefits, attended more carefully to his spiritual ministry, encouraged to hope that from it too they would receive corresponding benefits. It is a curious forecast of questions that are to-day so real in poor parishes.

Wilfrith was himself a banished man, and his friends and adherents had been banished too. They looked to him for support, as, five hundred years later, the banished friends of the banished Becket had to be maintained by him, a calculated meanness on the part of King Henry II., who with that intention banished them. Ethelwalch determined to provide Wilfrith with the means for maintaining his friends, and he gave him the promontory of Selsey. Here again, as at Bosham, you find that the local pronunciation gives the old force of Sels-ey, or Seals Island. As it then was, it was a land of eighty-seven families, joined to the mainland by a narrow neck, about a sling's cast across. There is still a very interesting causeway to drive over on the way to Selsey; "the island," as it is still called. The king made a complete and absolute gift of the whole, with all its possessions, lands, and men. Here Wilfrith founded the important monastery which remained to Bede's time. The priest Eappa governed it in Wilfrith's absence. Wilfrith performed the functions of bishop among the South Saxons, with this as his temporary seat, for five years; questions of "jurisdiction," whether local or œcumenical, do not appear to have troubled him or anyone else in England in those early times. After five years, the defeat and slaughter of Ecgfrith of Northumbria by the Cymri of Strathclyde opened the way for him to return home in 686. He had found among the inhabitants of Selsey, given to him by Ethelwalch, two hundred and fifty men and women that were slaves. He baptized and freed them all.

Had Wilfrith remained in Sussex, there might have been created in his person a South Saxon bishopric, with Selsey as its seat. As it was, the South Saxons were episcopally superintended by the West Saxon Bishop of Winchester for more than twenty years after his departure. In the year 709, as it chanced in the year of Wilfrith's death, though that had no connection with the event so far as we can see, it was determined by a synodal decree (of a West Saxon synod apparently) that the province of the South Saxons, which up to that time pertained to the diocese of Winchester, should itself have an episcopal seat and a bishop. Eadbert, the abbat of the monastery of Selsey, was consecrated the first bishop, and the monastery was the bishop's seat. He was succeeded by Eolla. When Bede finished his history, in 731, Eolla had been dead some years, and no one had been put in his place; the bishopric had passed out of existence. It was revived almost immediately after Bede ceased to write, in 733. There were twenty-two bishops of Selsey down to the Norman Conquest. The twenty-third bishop, Stigand (not the Stigand of Sherborne and Canterbury) became Bishop of Chichester, and at Chichester the bishop's seat has ever since remained. The old buildings of Selsey have long been covered by the encroachments of the sea; parts of the old church used to be visible on the east side of the "island" at low water, and boats still cast anchor in "the bishop's park." The two well-known ancient stone carvings in Chichester Cathedral are said by tradition to have come from the Cathedral Church of

Selsey; and on the whole their style does not deny the tradition, so far as date is concerned, though it cannot be said with confidence to confirm it.

When Wilfrith's work had been going on for about four years, Ethelwalch was slain. A certain very ambitious scion of the royal house of Wessex, Caedwalla by name, had been banished from Wessex. He thereupon came with his force of soldiers upon Ethelwalch of Sussex, defeated and slew him, and wasted the territory. He was driven out by the king's commanders, Berthun and Andhun, who for some time held the reins of government. But Caedwalla became King of the West Saxons the next year, and he then completely subdued the province of Sussex. He took, also, the Isle of Wight, the last great stronghold of paganism, and set himself to slaughter all the inhabitants and fill their place with emigrants of his own race. He had vowed, though not himself a Christian, so Bede understood, that if he conquered the island he would give to God the fourth part of the land and of the plunder. He fulfilled his vow by giving to Wilfrith land of three hundred families, the whole island being a land of twelve hundred families. Wilfrith had almost immediately to leave for the north, and he committed the charge of his newly acquired property to one of his clergy, Bernwin, his sister's son, giving him a priest, Hiddila, to minister the word and baptism to all who might wish to be saved. Two years after Wilfrith's departure, Caedwalla gave up his kingdom and went to Rome. There he was baptized on the 10th of April, 689; and ten days after he died. He was buried in St. Peter's at Rome, and the Pope (Sergius) had an epitaph in twenty-four elegiac verses set up over him.

It is in connection with this gift of the Isle of Wight that we have the very pretty story of the two brothers of Atwald, king of the island. They had escaped from the slaughter, and sought refuge among the Jutes on the mainland, in Hampshire as we should say. They were conducted to a place called "at the stone," there to be concealed, as they believed, from the conqueror; but, instead, they were betrayed, and they were ordered to be slain. This became known to Cynebert, a priest, and abbat of the monastery of Reodford, the Reed-Ford, probably the modern Redbridge near Southampton. He made his way to the king, then being nursed for wounds received in his invasion of the island, and begged that if they must be put to death he might first convert them to Christianity. The king gave him leave. He taught them, baptized them, made them certain of entry to the kingdom of heaven. The executioner came, and they joyfully went to death. These were the firstfruits to God of the Isle of Wight, the latest province of all England to depart from idolatry.

We have seen[1] that Wulfhere gave to the king of the South Saxons not only the Isle of Wight but also the district of the Meonwaras in Wessex. The Meons in Hampshire still retain the ancient name in the villages of Meonstoke and Eastmeon. One of the churches in that neighbourhood, Warnford, near Bishop's Waltham, has an interesting record of Wilfrith's work there, in an inscription about two or three generations later than the Norman Conquest, setting forth that Adam de Port renewed the church, which Wilfrith had founded[2]. Hugh de Port was a very large landholder in these parts at the time of the Domesday Survey.

---

[1] See pp. 62, 165.
[2] There are two inscriptions, one on the front of the

There is another pretty little story, about a boy in the monastery at Selsey. Bishop Acca of Hexham told it to Bede, and Acca had had it told to him by most credible brothers of the monastery. The great plague which made such havoc in several of the English kingdoms about the year 682, the second pestilence with which we have had to do in these lectures, reached at last to the monastery governed by Wilfrith's priest Eappa. Many of the brethren died, both of those who had come with Wilfrith and of those who had been converted on the spot. A fast was proclaimed.

There was in the monastery a young boy, recently called to the faith. He was seized with the plague on the second day of the public fasting and prayer. As he lay alone,

---

porch, the other on the north wall. Canon Benham has kindly given me the exact words:—
    (1) Fratres orate prece vestra sanctificate
        Templi factores seniores et juniores
        Wilfrid fundavit bonus Adam renovavit.
    (2) Adam hic de Portu solis benedicat ab ortu
        Gens cruce signata per quem sum sic renovata.

(1) Brothers, pray; sanctify with your prayer the builders and the re-builders of the church. Wilfrith founded it; the good Adam rebuilt it.

(2) Let the race that is signed with the sign of the cross here bless from the rising of the sun Adam of Port, by whom I am thus rebuilt.

there appeared to him the most blessed princes of the apostles. They bade him not fear death, for they were that day to take him to heaven; only he must wait till the mass was celebrated, that he might receive the viaticum of the Lord's Body and Blood. And they assured him that no other in the monastery should die, only he; for the religious King Oswald, of whose death that was the anniversary, had interceded for them. This the boy told to a priest. The priest looked in the calendar, and found that it really was the anniversary of Oswald's death. He asked what was the appearance of the two men that had come to him. The boy could never have imagined men so fair to look upon. One was shorn like a clerk; the other had a long beard. They had told him that the one of them was called Peter, the other Paul; and that they were ministers of our Lord and Saviour Jesus Christ, sent by Him from heaven to protect the monastery. The boy died on the same day. It is very interesting to notice that in each of these little earliest English historical tales, the conception of a happy ending to the tale was an early Christian death. The placing together of St. Peter and St. Paul as the two princes of the apostles, as of equal dignity and power, as equally representing Christ upon earth, so far as any apostle did represent Him, is true to the facts of early history and early art. The cult of St. Peter and St. Paul is the early fact, the cult of St. Peter is later. Rome was the Apostolic See, because it was fertilised with the blood of St. Peter and St. Paul. It was to visit the sepulchres of "the apostles" that our early ancestors went to Rome; it was in the name of St. Peter and St. Paul, in the authority of St. Peter and St. Paul, that the Popes on great occasions spoke, as, for instance, in cursing root and branch the Great Charter of the liberty of England[1]. The martyrology of Gorman has on June 29 *Petar Pol ar primchind*, "Peter, Paul, our leading chiefs." There the true voice speaks.

Ethelwalch the king, and Wilfrith the bishop, will appear in our transept windows as representing Sussex. For Kent, which I have not had an opportunity of mentioning, we shall have Ethelbert as the king and Augustine as the archbishop. And we add Theodore, on account of the importance of his work.

---

[1] See also p. 53. I have explained in the preface the retention of statements which have appeared in other parts of these lectures.

We have now run through all the kingdoms of the English Heptarchy, and have seen how each was brought to Christ. Of all the seven kingdoms there was only one, namely Kent, which owed its permanent conversion to the mission of Augustine directly, to pass by, as I think we decidedly must pass by, any work which the "French" bishop Luidhard may have done in the years preceding Augustine's arrival[1]. Of all the twenty-six counties of England there is only one, namely Kent, of which the same can be said, that it owed its permanent conversion directly to the mission of Augustine. East Anglia as a kingdom, Norfolk and Suffolk as counties, owe their permanent conversion to the labours of another foreigner from France; and his work was made possible by the conversion, in France, of the king through whom Christianity was restored after the relapse into paganism. Birinus, another foreigner, set the ball rolling in Wessex, but the work was done there by Scotic influence. Sussex, as we have seen this morning, was converted late in time, years after the close of the period with which these lectures have been concerned, by an

[1] See *The Church in these Islands before Augustine*, S.P.C.K., p. 10.

Englishman, brought up in Scotic Lindisfarne, but devotedly attached to the Roman Church. And even there the Scotic Church had taken possession and was quietly at work, before Wilfrith had ever preached in those remote parts. And years before Wilfrith's arrival, the king had been converted and baptized in Mercia. There was no Canterbury mission to Sussex. With these few exceptions England owed its final and permanent conversion to the labours of the Scotic Church. Thus, while Gregory and his mission were undoubtedly the founders of the Christian Church in England—using that word, of course, to describe the English part of the island after it had ceased to be inhabited by Britons—the founders; that is, of the Church of England, they only laid the foundation in the creation of the Kentish Church, and on that foundation they did not build. A phrase which I used two years ago still seems to me to describe the position which Gregory of Rome holds in connection with the origin of our Church. "He touched the spring that launched the Church of England[1]." Rome had very little

[1] See *The Church in these Islands before Augustine*, S.P.C.K., p. 155.

to do with the early navigation and the gathering way of the ship.

And it is not right to describe the Scotic Church as stirred up to the conversion of the English by the initiative of Gregory. It is quite certain that the conversion of Oswald and his brothers in Scotland, after their exile in 616, was carried out by the monks and priests from Iona independently of any action from Italy. The conversion of the rightful royal family of Bernicia may well have taken place before their cousin Edwin, rightful king in Deira and usurper in Bernicia, had formed the desire to marry Ethelburga of Kent, and had been brought under the influence of Paulinus. It was only the political conditions that prevented the Scotic Church from having the first hand in Northumbria; and we have seen how immense their success was when they did at last get their carefully prepared innings. We have seen, too, how their work told directly not only upon the whole of the English land north of the Humber, but also upon the whole of the middle of England down to Wessex, upon the whole of Wessex down to the south coast and across to the south-west as far as the Britons in Devonshire, and upon London with Essex and Middlesex. As all this flowed directly from the conversion in Scotland of Oswald and his brothers, the Scotic Church may fairly claim—if it were but alive to claim it—that its work in the conversion of almost the whole of England was primary, not secondary; was direct, not indirect; came of its own impulse, was not created by the stimulus of any of the three foreign missionaries, Augustine, Felix, Birinus.

So much of the Scotic Church. Some words must be said in this connection about the British Church, the Church of the Britons. There are many people who seem not to know that there was no continuity or indeed connection between the British Church and the Church of England in the early centuries of their joint existence. A vague idea appears to be abroad that the British Church, the Celtic Church, the Scotic Church, were practically all one, and that the British Church can claim its part in the credit of the Scotic Church. The British Church had nothing whatever to do with the conversion of England, of the English; nothing to do with the origin or early work of the Church of England. From first to last, as far as I can remember, the two British bishops whom

Wini got to help him in the consecration of Chad are the only link we have with the British Church in any of the times of which we have been speaking. And there emerges from this complete absence of connection a rather interesting set of considerations.

If, as the modern Roman tells us, the original Christian Church of this island, the Church of the Britons, was really founded by Rome, the Roman Church (as Gregory described the Church of his nation, just as he called our Church the English Church) the Roman Church had behaved very badly to its child. It had completely deserted it; had let it drift—no one can suggest how—into uncatholic practices; had let it so completely lose all knowledge of its parentage, that in or before the year 600 it declared in the most contumacious manner that it would have nothing to do with Rome or its representatives.

It is to me perfectly clear that no claim to have founded the British Church was believed at Rome in those days, notwithstanding the late insertion in the early Chronicles of the story of Lucius and Eleutherus. When Gregory sent Augustine to the English without any mention of British bishops, or a

British Church, or a British people, it seems impossible that he knew of the fact that the British Church, and bishops, and people, were a highly important factor in the island which he seems to have regarded as pagan. And when Augustine found out that there were British bishops in considerable numbers (indeed their numbers were larger than his own succession ever at any one time attained to), and wrote to Gregory about them, it is inconceivable that Gregory should not in reply have said that they were children of Rome, if that was the fact. And when Augustine made his elaborate preparations for the interview with the British bishops, surely no argument he could use would have been so persuasive as this, that here was the long-lost mother, coming back in all affection to her long-forgotten child. When the Britons rejected his advances, they were clearly as completely ignorant of any ecclesiastical parentage which looked to Italy, as the Italians were of any claim of theirs as founder's kin. We may confidently trust the British bards to have kept the story alive, if, up to that time, it had ever lived. Even if Rome had forgotten her good deed—a thing not in itself very likely—for any such reasons as that

Britain was a small and far-off place and Rome had larger concerns, we may be sure that to the Briton—or shall we say the Welshman—an event of this character, directly affecting the Welshmen, would rank very high among the greatest events of the world. It would not be forgotten upon Cornhill while the Briton was dominant here; it would not be forgotten among the hills and the glens of Wales. At the Conference at Whitby, again, no such suggestion was made as that these islanders, British or Scotic, had ever owed allegiance to Rome, as ecclesiastical superior or as Christian founder; could trace anything at all to Rome; had any connection with Rome. This, it is unnecessary to say, brings the original Churches of Ireland and Scotland under the same argument of independence of Rome, under the same probability that the earliest Christianity was not due to Roman missions. The story on both sides at Whitby was quite the other way round. Colman and his party referred themselves to St. John the Evangelist, the disciple specially beloved of the Lord. Wilfrith referred himself to Rome, where, as he said, the blessed apostles Peter and Paul lived, taught, suffered, and were buried; he declared that in all the world nowhere but in these two islands, Britain and Ireland, were uncatholic practices as to Easter existent; and never, in his scathing and contemptuous argument, did he throw in their teeth any sort of suggestion that having once been taught better by Rome, they had fallen, in their insular isolation, into ignorance of the Catholic practice.

We owe to Gregory, Bishop of Rome, the great fact that under his magic touch the Church of England sprang into being. If he had lived we might have owed to him a good deal beyond this, in the guiding and guarding of the early life of the Church of England. And the Church of England might have been even better guided had he lived. But he died when Augustine died, and there was an end of practical help from Italy. Just when the growing Church in English lands needed very careful help and guidance, the helping guiding hand of Rome was removed. A whole generation passed away; nearly two generations. The weary old Italian Honorius remained quiescent at Canterbury, slowly dying out, and making no arrangements to continue his succession, which in fact died with him in 653. He knew, we may be quite sure, how the Church of the Scots, to whom he and his had addressed from time to time such superior letters, was faithfully doing the work that he and his had found themselves unable to do. And he must have thought sadly how little opposition there had been, to account for the little work that he and his had done. If he could have recalled the heroic death of one single martyr, he might perhaps have been able to say to himself that these were a dangerous, a desperate people. But not one single case had there been, so far as I know, of violent hands laid upon one of the Italians, unless we are to regard seriously the scourging of Laurentius. And even if we are, there are some difficult questions to be answered, as to who it was that really scourged him, under guise of St. Peter: no one suggests that it was an English pagan, and that Laurentius was to that extent a martyr. As far as I can see there was no excuse, no relief, no brightness, to comfort the soul of the last of the Italians, as he lay dying in his isolation at Canterbury. He looked forth upon the field which the great Gregory had intrusted to his predecessors, to his colleagues, nay to him personally. He saw it occupied to its widest extent. It was covered with Christian labourers. But they were labourers not of his sending, the ministers of a Church not his. When those of us who are alive in 1897 keep with full thankfulness the thirteen hundredth anniversary of the baptism of Ethelbert by Augustine of Rome, they will keep it with a zeal tempered with knowledge. They will not forget how relatively small a part that fact, so great in itself, really played. They will remember how much larger an area was covered in early times by the other great fact, the baptism of Oswald and of Oswy by the Scotic monks of Iona.

LECTURE VII.

THE BEWCASTLE CROSS, AND OTHER MONUMENTS.

The Bewcastle Cross, its ornamentation.—The Kirkdale sundial.—The chair of Maximianus.—Interlacements: Anglian, Hibernian, Italian, and Lombardic.—The Runes.—Runic inscriptions on the Bewcastle Cross.—Prayer for the soul on Anglian monuments.—Cross and inscription at Jarrow.—The Dedication-stone of Jarrow.—Persons named on the Bewcastle Cross.—Owin's monument.—The Cross of the holy James.

IF we were asked what princes they were that made the largest mark upon the times with which we have dealt in this course of lectures, say from 633 to 668; what princes they were that had most to do with spreading the Christian faith over England in those years and developing the Church of England; we should not have much doubt about the answer. Oswald of Northumbria; his brother Oswy; Oswy's son Alchfrith; and Wulfhere, King of the Mercians. The latest of these, Wulfhere, died in 675, one thousand two hundred and twenty years ago. We have still existing a great monument that masses together three of these names, Oswy, Alchfrith, and Wulfhere, and is shaped in resemblance and remembrance of the cross set up by the other of the four, Oswald. It was set up in the year 670, while Wulfhere was still alive, and it records the death of the other two, first Alchfrith, and then his father Oswy. It is the only source of our knowledge that Alchfrith was then dead.

This remarkable monument stands in the churchyard of Bewcastle, in the north-east part of Cumberland, about ten miles from the border of Scotland; twelve miles from Lanercost, from which place I drove across the country to visit it, and some nine miles from Gilsland. The fifty-fifth parallel of latitude passes near the present or the original home of all of the three greatest monuments of the kind which we English possess, and no other nation in Europe has such. They are the great cross at Ruthwell in Dumfriesshire, once Northumbrian, the great cross at Bewcastle in Cumberland, and Acca's cross at Hexham in Northumberland, now at Durham. Bewcastle is the place spoken of by Sir Walter Scott in Guy Mannering as a dangerous neighbourhood. It was on Bewcastle Moss that Dandie Dinmont was nearly murdered by the robbers. Down to the year 1830 or thereabouts it was said that only women were buried in the churchyard of Bewcastle, the men being usually hanged in Carlisle, for horse-stealing, sheep-stealing, and the like.

The monument in Bewcastle churchyard is the very noble shaft of a great cross. It is a monolith 14½ feet high from its pedestal. There is a socket at the top in which once stood the head of the cross. In Gough's *Camden* we read that a slip of paper was found in Camden's own copy of the *Britannia* (1607): "I received this morning a ston from my lord of Arundel, sent him from my lord William. It was the head of a cross at Bucastle." This was Lord William Howard, the "Belted Will Howard, who dwelt on the border." The Lord Arundel was Thomas, the first baron of Wardour, who took the Turkish standard with his own hand, fighting under Rodolph II, in 1595. The cross-head stood about 2ft. 6in. high, so that the monument when complete was 17ft. high, and with its pedestal it stood up nearly 21ft. from the ground. The head had letters across it which Camden could not read. His drawing of them shews us that they were runes;

3.—The Bewcastle Cross. South side, with east side in profile.

[*To face p. 191.*

but it is not accurate enough to enable us to read them with any certainty. The cross-head was blown out of its socket in a gale of wind. I have long lived in hope of finding it in some great house, or in some rubbish corner of a Museum.

One of the four faces of the monument, the east side, 22 inches broad at bottom and 14 at top, one inch more in each case than the two narrower sides, has a conventional trunk or branch of a tree running in graceful curves from bottom to top, passing across and across nine times, and each time throwing off a spiral tendril to occupy the semi-ellipse, ending in fruit at which a beast or a bird is nibbling. The whole is drawn in a very bold and skilful manner, and the animals and birds are full of life. Leaves and seeds and tendrils are thrown off freely in alternate directions, so as completely to occupy the field with ornament. This face of the shaft is shown in profile in illustration 3, on the opposite page.

It is quite impossible to see this beautiful sculpture without a wondering surprise. Who could have drawn, who could have executed in high relief, such a work of art as this, at any assignable date in Anglian history?

It represents, in all probability, the idea of a tree of life. The animals and the birds are peaceful and happy. This is in sharp contrast with similar representations on pre-Norman stones of later date. I have found, by removing some of the earth at the foot, that the great cross in Bakewell Churchyard has at the bottom of all a man with a bow, taking aim at the little creature nibbling the fruit at the top. At Bradbourne in Derbyshire there are the fragments of a cross equally noble with that at Bakewell; and there again on more than one side is a man at the foot taking aim at the squirrels or little foxes in the tree or vine. The great cross shaft at Sheffield has remarkable examples of the same kind. After the Conquest, this jarring note becomes still more conspicuous. Thus on the slight columns of the portals at the west front of Lincoln Cathedral, you have in alternate circles animals and men with spears attacking them. The whole idea of peace has perished in the idea of sport or of slaughter. See appendix A, p. 223.

The west side is in three divisions or panels. This face is shewn in illustration 4 (frontispiece). Unlike the east side, it has inscriptions, of which I shall speak later. At the top is a noble figure of a Saint with a nimbus, carrying a Lamb with a nimbus, presumably John Baptist. Next below, with a short inscription between, is a still more noble figure of Our Blessed Lord, with a large nimbus; the right arm raised in the attitude of benediction, the hand unfortunately broken off; the feet are treading on the heads of swine. Next below is the principal inscription of the monument; and then, lowest of all, a man with hawk on left hand, and a wand in the right, with the hawk's perch, probably, occupying part of the field.

The other sides, north and south, are broken up into panels of irregular lengths, five on each side. Five of these, three on one face, two on the other, are occupied by interlacing bands in relief, all perfectly correct in principle, and at least one of them (the lowest panel on the south side, figure 3) exceedingly good in design, as good as any similar pattern in the Lindisfarne Gospels. Four of the remaining panels are filled with stiff foliage patterns, good in detail, but formal in general effect. Two of them are formed with one stem flowing from side to side as in the great panel already described, two are formed with two stems each, starting at opposite corners of the base of the panel, and in one case crossing, in the other meeting and returning. The one remaining panel (not seen in the illustrations) is nothing but simple chequers, perhaps the most difficult thing to explain on the whole cross, whether as to purpose or as to date.

In the upper of the two foliage panels on the south side (see illustration 3, page 191) there is the field of a sundial. A glance at the illustration will shew that it is contemporary with the sculpturing of the scroll of foliage. It is of course on the south side, and as the shaft stands on the south side of the church, the sun strikes it full and clear. We have a considerable number of Anglo-Saxon sundials remaining, some of them with Anglian inscriptions, in those northern parts. The most interesting of all is that at Kirkdale Church, near Kirby Moorside, of which I have spoken [1] as possessing the two remarkable sepulchral slabs which I assign to King Ethelwald of Deira and Bishop Cedd of Lastingau and of the East Saxons. This Kirkdale dial is so remarkable that I will make a digression to describe it.

[1] See pp. 151, 152.

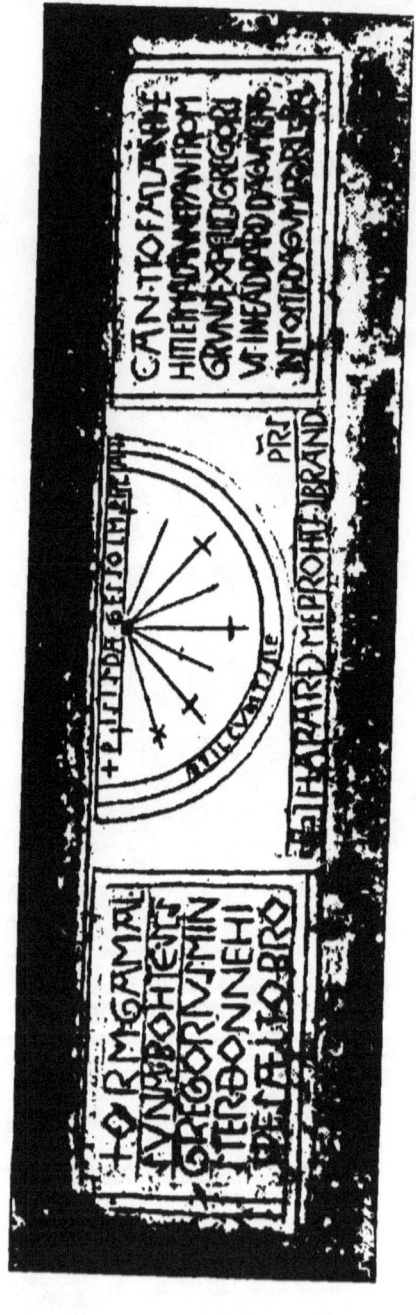

5.—The Sundial at Kirkdale Church.

The inscription, as will be seen from illustration 5, opposite, is as follows :— + This is dages sol merca æt ilcum tide + 7 haward me wrohte 7 brand prs. *This is the sun's mark at every time, and Hawarth wrought me and Brand the priest* (or, possibly, the *provost*; it is not certain what the abbreviated form *prs.* means). Bransdale, it may be remarked, is still the name of a dale not far off, between this and Stokesley. Then comes a lengthy inscription, of unique interest and value: it is placed on two stones, one on each side of the dial, just as the dedication of Jarrow Church is inscribed on two stones :— + Orm Gamal suna bohte Scs Gregorius minster ðonne hit wes æl tobrocan 7 tofalan 7 he hit let macan newan from grunde Xre Scs Gregorius in Eadward dagum cng in tosti dagum eorl+. *Orm, son of Gamal, bought St. Gregory's Minster. Then it was all broken and fallen to. And he made build it new from the ground for Christ and St. Gregory in the days of Edward king in the days of Tostig earl.* Orm and Gamal were names fatally connected with the misdeeds of Tostig and his banishment from Northumberland, to the results of which the failure of Harold at Hastings is to be attributed.

It will be seen that there is a cross incised on the line of shadow which marked the time for the morning service. This is not infrequent on early dials, but the place of the cross is not always the same. At Kirkdale it is one-fourth of the way between sunrise and noon, that is, about 9 a.m. at midwinter, and about 6 a.m. at midsummer.

To return to the Bewcastle Cross. If we ask where in the world these ornamental patterns could at that time come from, the archæologist will tell us that the four foliage patterns are stiff examples of classical art. The great flowing scroll with the animals and the birds nibbling the fruit is as much the opposite of stiff as anything can be. I suggested, some years ago, that it was very difficult to look at the noble ivory chair of Maximianus, which they shew you with so much proper pride in the sacristy of the Duomo of Ravenna, without feeling that on the uprights on either side of the front of the chair you have the secret of the original of this most beautiful side of the Bewcastle Cross. That chair had been in existence about a hundred years when the Bewcastle Cross was set up, and either it, or the original design from which its ornament was in its time taken, or something very closely allied to it, must certainly have been in the mind of the designer of the Cross. See appendix B, p. 224.

As to the interlacing patterns, the question is more difficult. Our Hibernian friends claim that the whole of this art came from them. But they have no stone-work of anything like the date of the Bewcastle Cross with anything like these patterns. Their earliest great Cross, too, dates from 920 only[1], that is to say, 250 years later than this Bewcastle Cross. If it is claimed that the Irish parchment ornamentation gave the patterns of these panels of interlacing ornament, we have to reply that we are not aware of any MS. of Irish production with these patterns so early as the year 670. The distinctively Hibernian patterns, whether for the ornament of metal work or for the ornament of parchment, are markedly absent from the Bewcastle Cross, and emphatically absent from the other English Crosses of the earliest date next to it. It is not impossible to claim these intricate and effective patterns as a development due to the artistic ingenuity of the

[1] The Flann Cross at Clonmacnois, and the very similar cross at Monasterboice, are of this date, within a year or two.

Anglian race, a development from rudimentary ornament of the same character, used by their European ancestors and cousins, akin to the rudimentary ornament found among the Burgundians and the Franks. But there is more to be said in favour of these patterns also having come from a land of classical art. We find plenty of examples in Rome—they have found scores more since I was in Rome eight and a half years ago—of marble screens covered with ornament in relief which looks like the Anglian interlacing work, and was being done in Rome in the seventh century. But it is entirely different from ours in principle, being produced by a repetition of a number of isolated forms, quatrefoils and so on, linked into one another so as to give the effect of a continuous band forming reticulations. With our early Anglian work that is never the case; we proceeded by the convolutions of continuous lines, not isolated circles and quatrefoils superposed on one another. It is, generally speaking, only in Lombardy that we get in early work in Italy the continuous endless bands which form the basis of the beautiful surface ornaments of our Anglian ancestors. There were of course famous Irishmen in

Lombardy; and it used to be said that they introduced this ornament there. But in very recent times the ornamentation of the tomb of St. Columbanus himself, the very test case, has been brought out from its obscurity; and it proves to be an exact counterpart of that found in Rome, and entirely different in principle from that found in Northumbria. Considering the date of Columbanus—he died at Bobio in 615—that may be accepted as conclusive proof that it was not the Irishmen who produced, and introduced into Lombardy and elsewhere, these beautiful endless mazes. I must not wander into the delightful field which the Lindisfarne school of ornament of Anglian times affords; nor go now to Byzantium. See appendix C, p. 226.

Of the figure of our Lord on the west side of the Bewcastle Cross, a figure about three and a half feet high, I can only say that a more dignified simplicity could not be given to such a figure in any age. I have had it put on glass, and shewn by limelight on a screen, the full size of life. It never fails to impress deeply an audience, of whatever class. Nothing that I have seen of early sculpture in foreign museums has produced the same kind of effect on myself; and the effort to conceive its being produced in Cumberland 1225 years ago, whether by native, or by Gallican, or by Roman masons, is merely bewildering. It is still more difficult to imagine its being done at any later date consistent with the obvious facts. There was just at that time in the north of England a coincidence of devoted love for the best ecclesiastical ornament of the centre of the Church of the West, with the presence of artists able to design better work than the Romans.

It is time now to come to the inscriptions on this remarkable monument. They are all in Runic letters, decidedly Anglian Runes, differing, in conspicuous respects, from the typically Scandinavian Runes. I do not think that sufficient notice has been taken of this difference, and of what it must mean. For myself, I derive the Runic alphabet from the forms of Greek letters which prevailed four or five centuries before Christ. Others derive them from an early Latin alphabet, so early as to be very closely akin to the Greek, even more closely than the ordinary Latin capital letters are akin to the ordinary Attic capitals. In either case the Runic letters are little more than variants of these early capitals, altered so as to make them easy to cut on the surface of wood, especially a wood that splintered. Vertical lines, which are easily cut against the grain, and diagonal lines, which are sufficiently against the grain to be cut with comparative ease, are universal. A horizontal line, which it is so difficult to cut along the grain of such a wood as deal without an awkward splinter at each end, never occurs in the Runic alphabet. And curved lines, as in the capitals B and R, in almost all cases are broken into two straight lines meeting at a point. When the Runic letters, formed originally for convenience of cutting on wooden staves or tallies, came to be used for monumental inscriptions on stones, or, later still, for writing on parchment, the rule for breaking up a curved line into two straight lines was not strictly observed in all cases. The important thing for us to notice is, that where the Anglian Runes differs from the Scandinavian Runes, the Anglian is nearer to the early Greek (or early Latin) original. This gives, I think, a flavour of antiquity to the European cradle of our Anglian race, which has not been sufficiently noticed; indeed, I do not know that it has been noticed at all. I use the word "Anglian" throughout, because the existing Runic inscriptions in England, of which there are twenty or more, are in the Angle lands, not in the Saxon. There is one word in Runes at Sandwich, and one word at Dover. And we have of course the very remarkable late Runic stone of the time of Canute, dug up here in St. Paul's Churchyard, with its Scandinavian Runes telling us that "Kona caused set up this stone and Tuki." The rest of the Runic inscriptions are in the north.

On the Bewcastle Cross we find the earliest examples, known to be in existence, of English literature. On the last leaf of our Cambridge manuscript of Bede's *Ecclesiastical History*, written in Bede's lifetime, there is, on the back of the leaf, in a small hand probably contemporary, the English version of the beginning of Caedmon's first song, which in the body of the MS. is given only in Latin. But that, even if it is contemporary, is not earlier than 731, sixty years later than the date of the Bewcastle Cross. This fact, that we have here the earliest known specimen of Anglian script, of English literature, is enough to give a unique position to this great monument of antiquity.

Beginning with the west side [1], there is at

---

[1] Figure 4, frontispiece.

top, just where the blowing out of the socket of the actual cross head has injured the edge of the socket, one word, perhaps " Kristtus." Then, above the head of our Lord, in two lines, with an initial cross, " Gessus Kristtus," *Jesus Christ*. This at once gives us the *y* pronunciation of the Anglian *g*, and shews us that our Anglian ancestors pronounced their consonants *s* and *t* very sharply and decidedly in the middle of a word, practically doubling them. Then, above the head of the king, if a king it be, comes the main inscription, which tells us who it was in memory of whom this monument was raised, and who set it up; and telling us more than that. The runes read as follows:—

+ " This sigbecn thun setton hwætred wothgar olwfwolthu aft alchfrithu ean küning eac oswiung + gebid heo sinna sowhula."

+ "*This thin token of victory Hwætred Wothgar Olwfwolthu set up after* (in memory of) *Alchfrith once king and son of Oswy.*" Then,

"*Pray for the high sin of his soul.*"

Here, then, we have the monument of the sub-king Alchfrith of whom we have heard important things in these lectures; the son of Oswy by a Celtic marriage; leaning naturally to the Scotic Church; settling at Ripon a colony of Scotic monks; then coming under the influence of Wilfrith; turning out the Scotic monks because they would not conform to his new views, and putting their adversary Wilfrith in their place; finally, the main mover on the Catholic side of the Conference of Whitby, where his father Oswy and he sat as king and sub-king. We shall see by the other inscriptions that the Cross was set up in 670, six years after the Synod of Whitby, so that Alchfrith was dead by that time. We have already remarked, in speaking of the great part which Alchfrith played in the conversion of Peada of Mercia, that Bede drops him after Whitby in a very mysterious manner, only remarking that he gave his father much trouble. We have from no historical or traditional source any idea how or when he died. But here, in this imperishable record, we learn that he was dead in 670, and that his soul was burdened with some high sin. This may well account for the silence of Bede. I will not venture upon the many suggestions which crowd upon the historic imagination.

One thing must be specially noticed. This

6.—Tombstone and Runic inscription at Thornhill, near Dewsbury.

earliest piece of English literature, this earliest English sepulchral inscription, contains a request for prayer for the sin of Alchfrith's soul, and Alchfrith was dead. This is quite in keeping with the other records of the earliest Anglian times, whether English people of to-day like it or not. Here are examples:—At Thornhill [1], near Dewsbury, + *Gilsuith raised in memory of Berhtsuith a token at the grave-mound. Pray for the soul.* At Lancaster, *Pray for Kynibalth.* At Falstone, *Pray for the soul.* At Upton [2], *The people set up the memorial. Pray for Ethelmund.*

We must also note the description of the cross as a "token of victory." Thirty-six years before this, Oswy's brother Oswald had set up, at a place about twenty-five miles off as the crows fly, a wooden cross as the sign under which he determined to fight for victory. And the victory in that sign he won. And Bede tells us that up to that time no cross had been erected in Bernicia [3].

---

[1] See figure 6, opposite.
[2] See figure 7, p. 206.
[3] This was expressly limited to Bernicia. In the time of Edward I. there were still standing near Easingwold crosses quoted in a charter as a landmark, under the name of Paulinus's Crosses. That was in Deira.

It would be to shut our eyes wilfully if we failed to see in this Bewcastle inscription an evident reference to the great victory of Oswy's and Alchfrith's race, won under the sign of the cross. There is no doubt a deeper reference, to the victory of our Lord on the cross. It is this note that is struck in the Anglo-Saxon poem of the *Dream of the Cross*, several stanzas of which are inscribed in runes on the great Cross at Ruthwell, so similar to this of Bewcastle. One of the lines of that poem, not hitherto supposed to be included in the parts inscribed on the cross, declares of the cross, "This is no outcast's gallows." I have found on the head of the cross the word "gallows," and other suitable runes; and I believe that the cross had, in the upper parts where the runes are no longer legible, this stanza about the outcast's gallows. Indeed, it seems not impossible that this upper part, about five feet six inches high, was the original cross, and the great shaft, twelve feet high, was a few years later.

In connection with the use of the word token, or sign, or "beckon," it is worth while to mention a raised cross of early type on a slab at Jarrow, with an inscription in handsome sunk letters on each side of the shaft,

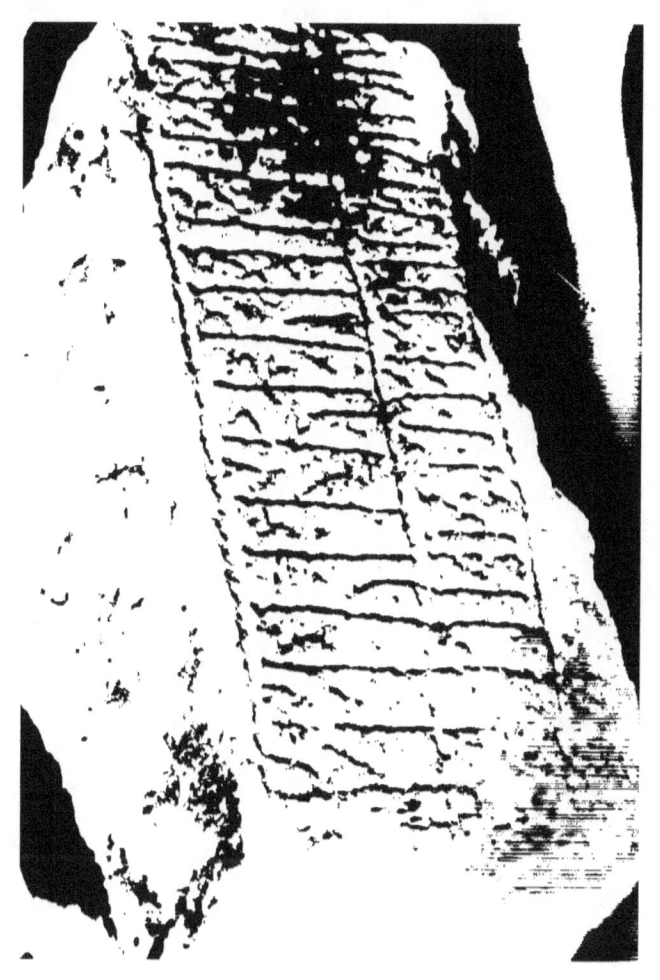

letters much too handsome and well cut to be

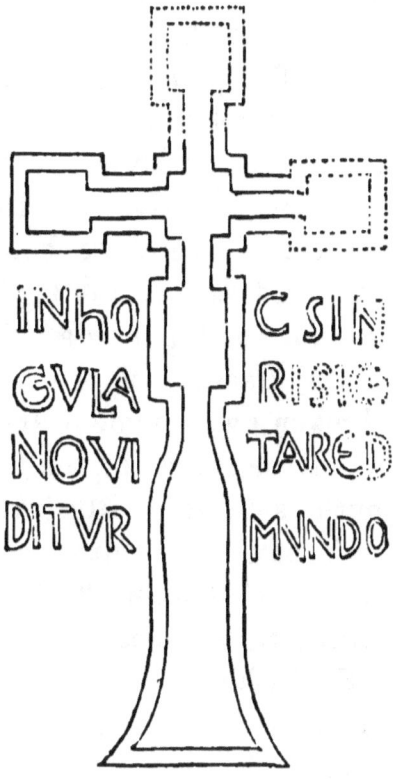

8. CROSS-SLAB AT JARROW.

late. The inscription is broken away at the critical point, as will be seen by the illustration 8 on this page. " In hoc singular[i sig]no vita redditur mundo,"—*In this sign alone*, or, *In this special* or *unique sign, life is restored to the world.* See also appendix D, p. 229.

We now come to those parts of the inscriptions which are in some senses the most important. The south and north sides, as we have seen, are divided into five panels each. The panels have ornament in relief on a sunk field, and this leaves a horizontal border between each two panels, where the original surface of the stone is preserved. On these borders there are runes inscribed, and all are legible except some of those on the top border of the south side, where the fracture of the edge of the socket has broken away some of the letters.

Beginning at the lowest of the five borders on the south side (see illustration 3, at page 191) we have: "Fruman gear," *First year;* on the next border "Küninges," *Of the king;* next, Rices thæes, *Of this realm;* and next, "Ecgfrithu," *Ecgfrith.* Here, then, we have the date. Not Alchfrith only but his father Oswy, is dead; and this monument is erected in the first year of Oswy's brother and successor, the warrior Ecgfrith. That year is 670 A.D.

This is not our only contemporary monument which bears Ecgfrith's name. The dedication-stone of the Church of Jarrow, to which I have already referred, dates itself in 685 by his fifteenth year, as the Bewcastle

9. The Dedication Stone of Jarrow Church.

Cross dates itself in 670 by his first year. The inscription[1] is in Latin, and in Latin letters, on two stones, now placed one below the other: "Dedicatio basilicae sci Pauli v.IIII k͞l mai anno xv Ecfridi reg | Ceolfridi abb ciusdem q' eccles d͞o auctore conditoris anno IIII." *The dedication of the basilica of St. Paul, on the ninth of the Calends of May, in the fifteenth year of King Ecgfrith, and the fourth year of Ceolfrid the Abbat, and under God the builder of the same.*

To return to the Bewcastle Cross. On the north side, beginning with the lowest border, we have "Künnburug;" next, "Küneswitha;" next, "Mürcna Küng," *King of Mercians;* next, "Wulfhere;" and, at top of all, three crosses and the word "Gessus," *Jesus.*

The Künnburug here named is Cyniburga, widow of Alchfrith, daughter of the famous pagan King of Mercia, Penda. It was this marriage that gave Alchfrith so much influence with Peada, Penda's son and sub-king; an influence which led up to Peada's baptism at Oswy's Court, and thus to the conversion of Mercia. Cyniburga retired eventually to her native Mercian land, and established

---

[1] See figure 9, opposite.

a church and monastery near Peterborough. It is now Caistor, famous for its noble church and interesting for its ancient remains. A ridge in Caistor Field is still called "Lady Cunnyburrow's Way." The dedication of the church is to "St. Kyneburgha," and it is said to be unique. It is a good example of a church taking its name at first from a living person, "Queen Cyniburga's Church;" then coming to be called in course of time "The Holy Cyniburga's Church;" and when "Holy" had been put into Latin, and the Latin *sanctae* was put into the more recent English "Saint," the Church becomes "St. Kyneburgha's."

We shall see, if we come to speak next winter, as is proposed, of the life and work of Wilfrith of Ripon and York and Hexham, we shall see how large his possessions were, abbeys and so on, in Northamptonshire. It is clear that this is to be accounted for by his great influence with Alchfrith, and with those relations of his by marriage whose names are on this Bewcastle Cross, especially Wulfhere. The records bear out this induction.

The other lady's name, Cyneswitha, may be that of Cyniburga's sister and companion at Caistor, who bore that name. The two sisters were commemorated together at Caistor; and soon after the year 1000 their relics were removed to the Abbey of Peterborough. The very remarkable stone shrine which still remains there is supposed to be theirs, if it is not that of Abbat Hædda, about 870. It is a difficult matter to decide between the two dates. I think myself the work is too good to be late; and those who make it post-conquest are in a position difficult to maintain.

On the other hand, the Cyneswitha of the Bewcastle Cross may be the mother of Cyniburga and Wulfhere, the widow of Penda. She bore that name. It was in her hands that Ecgfrith was held as a hostage, at the time of the great fight in which Penda at last was slain, in 655.

Finally, there is Wulfhere, King of the Mercians, Wulfhere who from 658 to 673 was one of the most powerful men in the English land; great as a fighting man, greater still as a Christian missionary king. Time after time, in the course of these lectures, we have seen him actively spreading the Christian faith, in his own kingdom and in the kingdoms of others.

I think we may with some confidence claim that looking to the importance in the history of the world of the conversion of England, and looking to the importance of these persons in the history of the conversion, there is no historical monument in these lands to compare with the Bewcastle Cross. And even if we pass into other lands, I do not know what monument has a like signal importance in connection with their conversion to the faith.

I will only ask you to consider at what date, later than that assigned by the cross, this monument can have been erected. First of all, it is certainly not a reproduction of a perished cross. The times that came after the Danish invasions were very dark times, and we cannot conceive any one setting to work to reproduce a great work of art like this. Within fifteen years of the date 670, every one mentioned, however incidentally, had passed away, and the interest in them had passed away too. Never from that time to this has there been an occasion on which such a reproduction would have had any relation to current events, or been in any way appropriate. Nor can we conceive of it as an original monument of later Anglian times, partly from the consideration thus stated, and partly from other considerations. Aldfrith, who succeeded Ecgfrith in 685, was a natural son of Oswy, and a favourer of the Scotic school and church, and a persecutor of Wilfrith. If Alchfrith had never left his first love for the Scotic Church, his half-brother Aldfrith might have set up a memorial of him. But Alchfrith was the head and front of the expulsion of the Scotic monks and priests and their practices. And if it was put up in Aldfrith's time, why should it be dated in the first year of Ecgfrith? Once get beyond Aldfrith's time, to attribute this monument, as an original, to any date and circumstance that can be mentioned or conceived is merely ridiculous.

There remains the idea of forgery. It was a well-known monument 300 years ago. From the Anglian times down to that time there was from the nature of the case no one in existence who had knowledge enough of early Anglian runes and early Mercian history even to write the inscriptions.

There is yet another monument which may with reasonable confidence be assigned to one of the actors in the times with which we have been principally concerned. Etheldreda, the daughter of King Anna, had married a prince of the Gyrvii, and received Ely as her marriage-gift. Her husband soon died, and in 660 she married Ecgfrith, who in 670 became King of Northumbria. She was accompanied to the north by her principal officer, the head of her household, by name Owini. Twelve years after her second marriage, she left Ecgfrith and eventually returned to Ely, and Owini is said by tradition to have been her steward at the principal manse of Haddenham. Some years ago, the base of the village cross at Haddenham, which had sunk deep into the ground, was dug out, and it was found to be inscribed with the words—"Lucem tuam Ovino da Deus et requiem,"—*give thy light, O God, and rest, to Owin.* There is an interesting account of Owini in the third chapter of Bede's Fourth Book, in connection with the death of Chad at Lichfield in 672. The date of Owini's death we do not actually know. The stone is now in the nave of the Cathedral Church of Ely.

In the slight mention made in these lectures of persons present at the Synod or Conference of Whitby, James the Deacon was named as on the catholic side. Bede says of him, that when Paulinus fled from the north, on the death of Edwin, he left in his church at York

James the Deacon, a man ecclesiastical and holy, who remained long in the church and rescued from the old enemy much prey by his teaching and baptizing. He was very skilful in singing the services, and when peace was restored he taught many the art of church song after the manner of the Romans or the Cantuarians. He lived even to Bede's days (Bede was born about twelve years after the Synod of Whitby), and in Bede's time the village where he usually dwelled, near Catterick, was called by his name.

At Hawkswell, five miles from Catterick, there is the shaft of a cross in the churchyard which certainly takes us back to early Anglo-Saxon times. The shaft[1] is about four feet high, above ground, and it is covered with simple but unusual interlacing patterns, cut in relief, of the type so well known to those who have studied the curious and beautiful remains of Anglian art in the north of England. The commencement of the spring of the cross head can be seen at the upper part of the shaft. There is on the front of the shaft a small rectangular panel with raised border, and Hübner gives as the inscription (186) on the panel HAEC EST CRVX SCI GACOBI.

[1] See figure 10, p. 216.

216　THE BEWCASTLE CROSS,

10. THE CROSS OF THE HOLY JAMES.

Whitaker [1], writing in 1828, gives a drawing of the cross, with a panel but with no sign of an inscription. The local guide-book says positively there is no inscription. The panel is about 3½ × 2 inches, and with the exception of a possible o there is no appearance remaining of an inscription. By rubbing with a soft pencil on tissue paper, some of the letters can be detected, notably the "Irish" or "Anglo-Saxon" G. A "squeeze" shews five or six of the letters fairly clearly, and the G quite unmistakeably. The Rev. C. E. Wyvill, Rector of Spennithorne, has lent me a very valuable tracing of a copy he made of the inscription thirty years ago, when he was Curate of Hawkeswell in Mr. Pattison's time. It agrees with Hübner's inscription and with the squeeze, except in the initial letter of *Jacobi*, which it gives as a long I. The late Rev. D. H. Haigh published the inscription in the *Archaelogia Aeliana* in 1856, from impressions sent him by Miss Pattison, the daughter of the then Rector, and he was Hübner's informant. Gale, knowing nothing of the Hawkswell Cross, suggested that "Ackburgh," between Tunstall and Hunton, meant *Jacobi burgus*, and was the place referred to

[1] Hist. of Richmondshire, i. 323.

by Bede. Whitaker made merry over this, and confuted Gale by stating that "Aikburgh" meant the burgh of the oak, and that to support Gale's view it ought to be "Jakeburgh." Mr. Moberley, in his notes on Bede, knowing nothing of the cross, quotes without disapproval Murray's statement that it is tolerably certain that the first syllable of Akeburg has no connection with *Jacobus*.

There is no place or village called Akeburg between Tunstall and Hunton, and so far Gale was wrong. But he was not far wrong. Tunstall is two miles from Catterick, on the road which leads to Hawkswell, and Hunton is four and a half miles from Catterick, on a branch of the same road. A little more than a mile beyond Hunton is a single farm called on the ordnance map Akebar, variously spelled Aikbar, and held in the neighbourhood to take its name from oaks which grew there. When I got to the Hawkswell Cross, and found that the name on the panel really does begin with an "Anglo-Saxon" G, I remembered Bede's one word of the Angle language in his *Ecclesiastical History*, the *Gae* which Bishop John of Beverley made the dumb man say, *quod est lingua Anglorum verbum affirmandi et consentiendi*, our "yea," and also Bede's Adgefrin, now Yeverin, and I concluded that *Jacobi* was meant to be pronounced with a strong initial Y, and consequently with a short o. Accordingly I asked a labourer if there was any place in the neighbourhood beginning with Yăk, such as Yăkŏbur. I was told that "Yakbur" was the local pronunciation of Aikbar—said to be so spelled—a mile and a quarter away from the cross where I was standing, a single house by the side of the Leeming Beck, where tradition said a village had been long ago, no doubt the Ackburgh of Gale; but I was assured that "Yak" was an oak, as no doubt it is in Yorkshire when it is not the first syllable of Jacob-burg. The cross and the local pronunciation of Akeburgh or Ackburgh taken together seem conclusive in favour of the cross being the monument of James the Deacon, and the house by the water-side the site of his dwelling-place and the scene of many of his life-long baptizings. Bede, in speaking of Jacobus, uses the same epithet *sanctus* that we find on the cross[1].

The very close resemblance of the little

---

[1] With the *a* pronounced long and broad, like *aw* as in some parts of Yorkshire, Hauxwell or Hawkswell itself is very nearly "Yak's well".

panel, and of the inscription, to the well-known arrangement of the earliest Welsh stones of this type, would seem to indicate a British connection of some kind. It may possibly be that we have here a hint of some historical foundation for the account given by Nennius[1] of the baptizing of Edwin and twelve thousand men,—"if any one wish to know who baptized them, Rum map Urbgen[2] baptized them." This is more than the ordinary claim of the Briton to have done everything. It no doubt preserves a genuine tradition which assigned to a member of the royal family of the British kingdom of Rheged, on the north-west of Northumbria, a very large share in the original conversion of Northumbria. Taken literally, it would mean that Paulinus was himself a Briton by birth, educated in Rome. Two manuscripts of Nennius, of the 13th century, boldly say that Paulinus was this son of Urien. Short of that, it would mean that one of his chief assistants in the work, conceivably James himself, was of British origin. The coinci-

---

[1] Hist. Brit. 63.

[2] Or, Run map Urbgen, or Rimin ap Urbgen, according to other readings; "Rum" or "Run" or "Rimin", son of Urien.

dence of the name "Rum" or "Rimin" (the *i* being presumably pronounced as *u*) with the latinised form "Romanus," the name of the court chaplain present at the Synod of Whitby, may probably be accidental.

There is something very attractive in the idea which this cross thus suggests, emphasised as it is by the remark of Nennius, however little weight we may be able to give to any British claim made by the writer of that "history." It would be a novel pleasure to be able to think that the British Christians of Rheged, retaining as they so long did their independent sovereignty, were willing to take the knowledge of Christianity to their pagan neighbours, though the pagans had destroyed the Britons of the eastern principalities. This would not be inconsistent with the fact that six years later the great growth of the power of Edwin determined another British king to attempt the obliteration of the Angles. And it would be a satisfactory explanation of a difficult phenomenon, to be able to believe that it was a British prince whose voice—however italianised—spoke in their native language to the Britons remaining in the hills, told them of the faith their fathers and their mothers had held, and brought them down to the Glen and the Swale to be baptized into the old faith, while Anglian conquerors were being baptized into the faith that to them was new.

What, exactly, Bede may have meant when he said that James the Deacon lived to his times, it is impossible to say. He was a deacon in the year 627, and he may have been about the age of the century. If he lived to be eighty-five, Bede would be taken as a boy from Wearmouth to Jarrow about the time of his death. There is no difficulty, so far as the style of the monument is concerned, in the date thus suggested.

Close to Akebar, not more than two or three hundred yards away, is St. Andrew's Church, now used as the church of Fingall, a village some distance off. St. Andrew's at Rome, now St. Gregory's, was the home of Augustine and Paulinus, the abode of Wilfrith when in Rome; and, as we said last year, neither Augustine nor Wilfrith forgot St. Andrew in their English dedications. Hawkswell Church is dedicated to St. Oswald. Thus the Cross of the Holy James stands amid kindred memories, worthy of his faithful life and work.

Appendix A.

Page 192.

We are familiar with the idea of hunting and slaughter in connection with Roman scroll-work. My impression is that the peaceful instinct of early Christian art eliminated this idea, and that our earliest monuments in England were produced under that influence. Then the influence of the pagan work asserted itself, and the idea of peace was lost in the more mechanical copying of ancient examples which we find in "Romanesque" art.

A comparison of the birds and other creatures in the Bewcastle scrolls with those found in connection with scroll-work in Lombardy, is so very decidedly in favour of the Anglian examples, which are beautiful and full of life, that we must assign to our examples an early date and an artist of very unusual skill. The dignity of the human figures on the Bewcastle Cross is greater than that of any contemporary work in stone which I have seen anywhere else.

Appendix B.

Page 197.

I have mentioned the ivory chair of Maximianus as a work executed about two generations before the artist of the Bewcastle Cross became a student of art. There are two shafts, each more than seven feet high and about a foot square at bottom and ten inches at top, in the Archæological Museum (at the Brera) in Milan, which it is impossible to disregard in connection with the question of the originals of our great Anglian cross-shafts. They are from the long ruined church called the Church of Aurona, opened up this century in the course of excavations in the streets of Milan. On two capitals found among the ruins there is an inscription in Latin, *Here rests the Lord Archbishop Theodore who was unjustly condemned. Julian made me thus beautiful*[1]. These must have been the capitals of the columns which supported the sarcophagus of Archbishop Theodore of Milan, who

---

[1] "Julianus me fecit sic pulchrum." I am inclined to suspect a play upon the words "sic pulchrum" and "sepulchrum."

was murdered in 739. Thus the church itself, named after his sister, was a building of earlier date than that, and these two shafts may probably reveal to us the state of Christian art in Lombardy in the later part of the seventh century, about the time of the Bewcastle Cross. These shafts have on all four sides flowing scrolls, some double, forming ovals, the others single, as at Bewcastle, with tendrils passing off alternately left and right. The ovals contain leaf ornaments, the tendrils end in vine-leaves, grapes, &c. They have not birds and animals in them; but in one case there is a single bird at the top, and in the other case a single quadruped. These creatures are very rudely executed, as rudely as the quadruped on the Bakewell Cross; but all the rest of the work is beautiful. One of the shafts has a socket hole cut out at the top, and this may have served to hold a cross, but more probably they were shafts supporting columns, or (more probable still) an architrave.

Anyone who wishes to compare our Anglian work of this character with Roman work, can not do better than examine closely the Roman portal to the Chapel of St. Aquilinus in the church of S. Lorenzo in Milan.

There is the tree of life, of the cornucopiae character, with spiral tendrils, birds and lizards nibbling the buds of the tendrils, and *amorini* occupying the exterior spaces. In a second order there are stiff panels of foliage scrolls.

Appendix C.

Page 199.

In the five years of my tenure of the Disney Professorship of Archaeology in Cambridge, I lectured on the early sculptured stones of England, Scotland, Ireland, Cornwall, Wales, and Man. If I ever have time to publish the five courses of lectures, it will be seen what a very large amount of this early interlacing ornament we have in our islands, and how unique it is. The longer and further I press such investigations as I can make, the more I seem to see that we must look to a Greek origin for the outburst of this beautiful work in its highest perfection in Northumbrian England. In Rome, in the time of Wilfrith and Benet Biscop, there was none of it, speaking roughly. In Lombardy alone is it found in anything like the same perfection as in England. An examination of the remains in Lombardy, at Brescia and elsewhere, seems to shew that Greek artists from Byzantium, and not Italians at all, did this work, the Italians doing the work by isolated patterns as described in the text. The inscription on Acca's portable altar (he died 742) *hagie sophie* &c., the inscription on Cuthbert's portable altar (he died 687), and the Greek genitive on the wood work of the same, *in honorem S. Petru*, all point to a direct Greek influence in Northumbria towards the end of the seventh century. When we are told that Benet Biscop brought masons from Gaul, I am strongly inclined to think that they were men of Greek training, from the south of France, or perhaps from Cisalpine Gaul, and that through them the Lindisfarne school of ornament got its inspiration. The artistic taste of the Angles—as contrasted with the Saxons and the Jutes—seized upon the principles of the art, and carried them to their very highest perfection in such work as the Lindisfarne Gospels and some of the earliest Anglian Crosses. Aldhelm, as we know, brought over the Alps a white marble altar, sculptured with raised crosses, and this may be taken as a proof of the connection of our early art with Lombardy. There is now in S. Ambrogio at Milan, in the chapel of S. Satiro, a white marble altar which answers the description of Aldhelm's altar.

When we examine the fragments of interlacing work still surviving in Lombardy, we see that they are by no means always examples of the interlacement of continuous flowing bands. They not infrequently, it may be said usually, have the defects which the corresponding work in Rome and other parts of Italy shews. Thus even in Lombardy I think that the artists of the pure style were few, and their influence was brief. As for the British Islands, I more and more incline to think that by a happy accident the artist who came over with Biscop, and launched us upon our career of early Christian art, was one of the few masters of the pure style, a Greek by training if not by race. The most perfect piece of work left in Lombardy, of the pure style universal in the British Islands, is the famous peacock screen which served as a side to the steps up to an ambo in S. Salvatore at Brescia. The interlacing pattern which forms the border of the screen is the best pattern in Lombardy; and it occurs scores of times in our islands, both in its simple form as found in the peacock screen and in higher and more beautiful developments.

To attribute to the Angles the skill and imagination that would have been necessary for developing so rapidly their beautiful patterns from such rudimentary work as we find in Merovingian France, and in Scandinavian and other rude art of the earlier period, is practically out of the question. As for the "Irish" share in this particular kind of ornament at a date clearly prior to 670, I have failed to trace it.

Appendix D.

Page 207.

The inscription on the sides of the cross at Jarrow is usually supposed to have been " In hoc singulari anno vita redditur mundo," *In this remarkable year life is given back to the world.* In a paper read at Cambridge on October 20, 1884[1], I took that view, and my friend the Rev. W. T. Southward, Fellow of St. Catharine's College, made the ingenious

[1] See *Proceedings of the Cambridge Antiquarian Society*, 1884,–5.

suggestion of *signo* for *anno*. It is a question whether there really is room for the letters *sig*. The *g* is a large letter in this type, as is seen in the word *singulari*; and the remarkable crowding of the letters does not begin till a later point of the inscription.

There is a good deal that is interesting to be said of the reading *anno*. It is not unreasonable to suppose that there may have been a short inscription above the arms of the cross, the stone next above these, which carried the upper part of the cross, being no longer in existence so far as we know. It is conceivable that there may have been some indication of the year in which the cross was sculptured, either by reference to some known event, or by actual date as on the dedication-stone. The dedication-stone of the church states that the dedication was in the fifteenth year of King Ecgfrith and the fourth of Abbat Ceolfrith (A.D. 685). The letters of the inscription are of exactly the same size as those on the dedication-stone, and of the sixteen letters of the alphabet in the inscription fourteen are found on the dedication-stone and all in the same form, though three of them, A, E, and O, are found in two forms on the dedication-stone. Thus a connection between the two is very probable judging only from the two inscriptions. In assigning a meaning to the phrase " in this marked year life is restored to the world," after exhausting other suggestions, the idea of the cessation of some great devastation by plague or otherwise remains as the simplest and most probable. Bede (*Hist. Abb.* c. 8) says that Benedict Biscop made Eosterwini Abbat of Wearmouth and then went for the fifth time to Rome. He returned to find sad news. Eosterwini and a crowd of his monks had died of a pestilence which raged through the whole country. Bede tells us further (c. 11) that Eosterwini had been four years Abbat, and (c. 8) that Ceolfrith was made Abbat of Jarrow on the eve of Benedict's fifth visit to Rome and (c. 11, c. 12) that three years after Eosterwini's death Ceolfrith had been seven years Abbat. Thus the fourth year of Ceolfrith was the fourth year of Eosterwini, and the dedication of Jarrow Church took place in the year in which Eosterwini and a crowd of his monks died in a general pestilence, which is not mentioned after that year. Hence, in pious memory of the deliverance from the pestilence, *in hoc singulari anno vita redditur mundo*. It is well known that dedication crosses were usual from very early times; and William of Malmesbury, speaking of Aldhelm's dedication of Malmesbury Church a few years after this of Jarrow, says that it was usual to mark the occasion of a dedication by some *honorificum epigramma*. This last fact tells rather in favour of the reading *signo*.

It is an interesting fact (or probability) first pointed out by Mr. J. R. Boyle, that the stone, two feet square, with the inscription *Omnium Fil... Hadr.*, taken from the wall of Jarrow Church and now in the Black Gate at Newcastle, seems to have been placed like an oven shelf next above the stone under discussion, for it has on its edge the arms of a cross which must at least closely resemble those of the cross whose shaft is on the stone in the porch. The gauge is almost exactly the same, though not quite, and the cable moulding observable on the porch stone is carried across the edge of the Roman stone. The arms shewn in my illustration are from this Roman stone. They are of one of the forms which we should expect to find at that date in that district.

www.ingramcontent.com/pod-product-compliance
Lightning Source LLC
Chambersburg PA
CBHW031354230426
43670CB00006B/542